Mahanayak

Narendra Modi

Kumar Pankaj

DIAMOND BOOKS

© Publisher

Publisher : **Diamond Pocket Books (P) Ltd.**
X-30, Okhla Industrial Area, Phase-II
New Delhi-110020

Phone : 011-40712200
E-mail : wecare@diamondbooks.in
Website : www.diamondbooks.in
Edition : 2026
Printed by : Repro (India)

Translated by
V.A. Upadhye
Mahanayak Narendra Modi
By - Kumar Pankaj

Preface

Narendra Damodardas Modi is not an unknown figure anymore. The entire country has already been singing praises of his achievements. Narendra Modi has earned himself a new place of pride in the countries which have keen interest in India. His popularity has multifolded after his election as the Prime Minister of India. He is been seen as a Mahanayak.

This is also an acid test of how he will face and solve the challenges posed by the nation. This may not be new for him, as he has been regularly confronting challenges since his childhood. How is he going to channelize and give direction to the aspirations of millions of his countrymen to whom he has made promises during the pre-election campaigns? There are numerous intriguing questions as well as answers and solutions too because ever since he took the reins of Gujarat in his hands for the first time in 2001, he has not looked back. He became cynosure of the eyes of his citizens and after this he governed the state in 4 consecutive terms. His first and last tenure might have been brief but he has been immensely successful in winning the confidence of Gujarati population.

When Narendra Modi took the command of Gujarat in 2007, I observed during my travels that Gujarat was on a path of growth and development which was a gift of Modi's vision and relentless hard work to fulfil it. The people of Gujarat also had started to see and accept him as a visionary. At that time, I strongly felt that I must write about him. I spent a lot of time in compiling data and information which would enable me to write about him and thus my book 'Doordrashta Narendra Modi' was launched. This book became so popular among its readers that it was translated in many languages on popular demand. Its multiple editions were sold in bookshops and during the Parliamentary election campaigns of 2014; it reached to readers in a new version.

Narendrabhai Modi is the Prime Minister of the nation. There is no dispute that he has achieved all this through his brilliance, talent and single- minded pursuit of his goals through his dedication. His enormous willpower, positive thinking for the nation and relentless efforts for development and growth have made him a very popular leader and people look at him as an idol. BJP has created history in the leadership of Narendra Bhai Modi. For the first time in its history, it has achieved thumping and absolute majority; on its own. For the first time, at the swearing in ceremony of Prime Minister and his council of Ministers, not only the heads of neighbouring nations graced the occasion by their presence but many more world leaders arrived to wish him. The citizens of India witnessed such a golden historic moment for the first time in their life and it shall be long cherished by them. 'Acche din aane waale hai' has become a happy buzzword slogan on the lips of the large population of this country.

Now the faith shown by millions of the countrymen in electing him has to be justified by him and their aspirations have to be realised. I have discussed in great detail about Narendra Modi, the man and his qualities in various chapters of this book. I have also narrated about the proper utilization of media and social media. The Prime Minister has to face many challenges and time alone will tell how he is going to handle them, but one thing is sure that a man who has a single minded thought, a vision and a purpose, he is Narendra Modi who is now the Prime Minister. And this thought will help this country and its common man to move in the direction of progress.

To conclude, I am thankful to publisher Shri Narendra Verma who already had identified the greatness in Modi long ago. He has been spreading Modi's messages and thoughts through the medium of Diamond Publications all along. I am also thankful to my well-wishers who gave me valuable suggestions from time to time during the launch of newer editions of the book and encouraged me so that I felt inspired to continue with my creative work. This book is now available to all my readers due to their valuable support and contribution.

-Kumar Pankaj

E mail- kpankaj31@gmail.com

Contents

Acche din aane waale hain

The most discussed and appealing slogan of BJP for the Parliamentary Elections is "Acche din aane waale hain" (Good days are sure to come). This is on everyone's lips. Even in the normal day to day conversations, everyone keeps repeating that whatever one may say, good days are sure to come. Therefore, Narendra Modi while commenting on BJP's win, said, "This is the win of India, good days are sure to come."

BJP has won, good days are sure to come. This is the best performance of BJP in the Parliamentary Election so far on its own. Prior to this, the best, so far, was in 1999 when it won 182 seats in the Parliamentary Elections. At that time, the party had formed an alliance under the leadership of Atal Bihari Vajpeyee under the banner of National Democratic Alliance (NDA). Modi had twitted, "India has won and this win is going to bring good days." Modi has a right to proclaim this with confidence because what he achieved in Gujarat was not only lauded in India but all over the world. Through the campaign medium of Vibrant Gujarat, the news of Gujarat's outstanding progress had reached to every nook and corner of the world.

Today, the hopes and aspirations are getting fulfilled far beyond their expectations. Gujarat is leading the way through e-governance, industrial direct investments, poverty eradication, power generation, SEZ, laying of roads and financial management. The prosperity of Gujarat is due to balanced growth in Agriculture, Industry and Service sectors. The greatest contributing factor in Gujarat's overall development has been his doctrine; 'Everyone's cooperation is everyone's development', his 'pro-people, pro-active governance (P2G2) formula in addition to active participation of people in its development. These have played an important role.

In spite of many obstacles, he resolved that the Narmada dam should reach to the height of 121.9 metres. He even resorted to fasting against the people who created obstacles in its path. To make many grids of several water resources in Gujarat, his initiative of Sujalam Suphalam Jal Sanrakshan Yojana (Water conservation scheme for prosperity) and to give it a direction for its proper implementation is a unique accomplishment.

His novel and first of its kind initiatives like Social Health Card, Roaming Ration Card shows his concern for the commonest of the common man. The multifaceted progress of Gujarat has been possible through Agriculture Festival (Krishi Mahotsav), Perennial Plan (Chiranjivi Yojana), Homage to mother (Matru Vandana), Save the daughter project (Beti Bachao Abhiyan), Light a lamp Scheme (Jyotigram Yojana) and Industriousness Movement (Karmayogi Abhiyan), e- affection (e – mamata), m-Power, Scope, i-create and many more schemes of this nature. In these days when the political leaders do not bother to see beyond the boundaries of the next elections, only a visionary like Narendra Modi can envisage such steps as a sincere politician for the future of generations to come.

In the capacity of an energetic and young leader, having novel ideas and who is acknowledged for his vision, Narendra Modi has been able to take his thoughts to his people from Gujarat with great success and has been able to win the trust and faith of more than 6 crore people there. His ability to remember even a common man by his name has won him love and affection of millions. He has been able to bridges between various spiritual and religious leaders on account of his immense respect for them. People from groups of different incomes, various religions and even people with contrasting political agendas have been respecting him as an efficient and far sighted visionary. He has been trying to bring upliftment in the lives of masses through his transparency and concrete steps. He has won the hearts, love and affection of the people equally from rural and urban areas as an expert orator and policy maker. His supporters include people from every sect, religion and economic strata.

His proficient leadership has won many laurels and rewards for Gujarat. That include Sasakawa Award from United Nation for its Disaster Management Scheme, award from Commonwealth Association for Public Administration and Management (CPM) and UNESCO for Creative and Active Administration, CSI award for e- Governance etc. As a matter of fact Narendra Modi has won the best Chief Minister award from the general Public which itself prove his achievements.

The most impressive has been his Vibrant Gujarat programme which has been able to elevate Gujarat at the global level. Gujarat has become a preferred destination for all the overseas investors to set up industry. The 2013 Vibrant Gujarat Summit witnessed participation of 120 nations from all over the world which is a unique distinction in itself.

Gujarat has recorded **double digit** growth for last so many years. When Gujarat is surging ahead on the path of growth and progress, Modi is travelling tirelessly, leaving behind his foot marks, as a traveller and has transformed 'milestones' into 'smilestones'.

If we glance at his achievements right from the fulfilment of basic and fundamental needs up to his position as CM of the state, we see him clearly rising as an able leader and administrator.

If you want to see a fine amalgamation of new thoughts and idealism, then Modi is the right example of this confluence. His personality is an epitome of strong character, courage, dedication and far-sightedness which if emulated can take the youth of this country to dizzy heights of creative leadership. He has emerged as a role model for everyone. It is rare that leaders with tremendous enthusiasm, constancy of purpose also get enormous love from people in their public lives but Modi has gained all this. He has emerged as a powerful leader in a very short span of time and he holds tremendous potential to mould future. He has dreamt for setting up new cities which have modern infrastructure and facilities and which can take the nation ahead. Therefore he says, "Urbanization should be seen as an opportunity and not as a threat."

All along these years, India has been struggling with problems of inadequate and weak infrastructure. Due to lack of appropriate plannings, our roads are being overburdened with traffic and crowd.

At the same time, our public transport system is not very efficient. In addition to this, our cities are suffering from the shortage of recreational facilities. Imbalance in our plannings and a fast growing needs have been the main causes of problems in our cities and towns.

UPA government has been unsuccessful in eradicating the inadequacies and deficiencies in the infrastructure and also in raising above the common notion of formulating committees to solve the problems which span all over the nation. The entire focus is on implementing the plans but the results have been mostly unsatisfactory.

On the other hand, the NDA government under the stewardship of Atal Bihari Vajpeyee had brought revolution in the field of infrastructure development. Some of their achievements are listed below:

During their tenure of 5 years of government, NDA created 50 highways. They created the golden corridor of highways, started the national rural road scheme, a larger plan for rural connectivity, laid the foundation to interlink rivers, and implemented the open sky policy and also did work in the areas of privatisation and modernisation of airports.

Now Modi's thought process in context of infrastructure has come at a time when it is bound to prove as a sureshot remedy for our difficulties. He presented his point of view for the progress of the nation in the National Meet of BJP in Delhi which include the following–

Creation of 100 new cities, creation of satellite cities in the vicinity of large cities, network of Bullet trains, joining the rivers and similar projects which he considers to be a part of progress.

Normally, in any city, there are lot manythings related with infrastructure which have a direct bearing on the improvement in the standard of living of its citizens. These include public transport open public spaces, good roads etc. These are some of the unique features of Gujarat model has taken them ahead of many other areas. He has dreamt to take the nation ahead on similar lines of Gujarat model. Let us have a look at some of its unique aspects:

Let us see how the urban areas in Gujarat have been transformed and how people's comfort and convenience has been accorded top-most priority.

Public transport – Bus Rapid Transport System (BRTS)

When you walk on the roads of Ahmedabad, your attention is bound to be attracted to the city's most modern public transport; the Bus Rapid Transport System (BRTS). In comparison to many cities where BRTS has been unsuccessful, this public transport has proved to be a cost-effective to the citizens of Ahmedabad, comfortable and user-friendly way of commuting. This system has more than 60 buses which take care of people with special needs too. Since 2009, the public system (Jana Marg) i.e system for public (Janata ke Marg) has established itself as means of safe, comfortable and swift means of commuting for the citizens of Ahmedabad. This Public System gives priority to buses, pedestrians and non-motorised means of transport which is accomplished by separating all the motorised transport. On one hand, the buses ply in special lanes created in the center of the road; separate lanes have been created for cyclists and wide lanes for people walking on foot.

Sabarmati riverbank

The story of Sabarmati riverbank, of past few years, will demonstrate to you how a dry arid land which was used by children to play or used by circus owners to set up their tents has become pride of Ahmedabad. The Sabarmati Riverfront Development Project includes the 10.5 km stretch along banks of the river Sabarmati which includes 185 hectare reclaimed area .This also included Water Management Scheme for Flood Control and new network of sewer pipelines to clean the Sabarmati river. This has become a favourite recreation spot for the citizens of Ahmedabad who gather there after their hectic shedule at work. It has walkways, swings and other recreational facilities.

Kankaria Lake Development Project

Kankaria Lake which is right in the centre of Ahmedabad is the most attractive destination there but the lake was not developed adequately well to cater to the large number of people going there. The entire area was renovated under the Kankaria Lakefront Development Project led by Narendra Modi thus making it a major attraction for people from all over the world. Kankaria Lakefront's major attractions include Atal Express, Kids' City, Stone Mural Park, and the widely popular Kankaria Carnival which is organized every year in the month of December.

Surat Municipal Corporation Outer Ring Road Project

Looking at rapid growth of urbanization and the pressure it puts on the physical infrastructure in urban localities, need for expansion and new constructions cannot be underestimated. Keeping this need in mind, Surat has developed Outer Ring Road Project. Under this model, Surat Municipal Corporation (SMC) and Surat Urban Development Authority (SUDA) jointly prepared a five year plan of development of proposed road aimed at achieving a profit of Rs 11,960 crores. It means that these institutions will complete this project with an outlay investment of Rs 5,799 crores. The additional revenue can be used for projects like Rapid Transit System.

Ultra-modern Central Bus Terminal of Vadodara

In February 2014, Narendra Modi inaugurated the bus terminal in Vadodara which resembles an airport. This was the first terminal in India which is of international standard. The station has been constructed on the basis of PPP model and their walls depict the history of Vadodara through paintings and portraits. In 2012, with his unique thinking process, he addressed the bus drivers and said, "When more people use a ST terminal as compared with an airport, then why should a bus station not be like an airport complex?" Vadodara Central Bus Station holds a coveted position among all the other bus stations in India and it is glittering example of a new way of thinking. Its campus holds a supermarket, shopping mall, multiplex, restaurants and food court, business centre as well as a budget hotel.

In this model of Gujarat developmental progress these are few examples. Narendra Modi has translated the meaning of "Good times are sure to come" in no uncertain terms and communicated that the opportunity of leading the nation which is bestowed on him is not only for the benefit of Gujarat but for the entire nation.

India of the twenty first century

After BJP's magnificent win, while addressing the Victory Rally in Ahmedabad, Narendra Modi said that he will not let down the people and lose their faith. He promised that he will transform India into a nation which belongs to 21st century. He was so firm in his proclamation that the entire audience and the party workers present there broke into a thunderous applause. Modi never works with hatred or malice in his heart. Therefore, he says that he would not resort to any kind of malicious behaviour even with his rivals who lost the elections. He wants to take along everyone including the opposition parties with him. Modi said that this was the first time in his election campaigns where he did not hold any rally in Ahmedabad before the elections and there lies his success. He puts forth the logic that people who fought the elections on the basis of vote bank politics and not on the basis of development as their election agenda whereas he fought the elections with development and good governance as his manifesto. The Youth broke away from casteism and they rose above the casteist politics and cast their votes. Modi's speeches clearly convey that the days of politics of dividing the voters to win the elections were the tactics of the past and a new dawn of uniting them has set in. A new Socialist outlook is emerging. He said that for the first time the citizens of India have provided an opportunity to form a single party Government with a huge mandate.

Modi says that it is the strength of Indian democracy that it provided an opportunity to a lad from a poor family to contest the elections and in the process he became the cynosure of everyone's eyes. People have every right over him. He will never let them down and betray their faith. He wants to promise the countrymen that he would never hurt their sentiments and faith instilled by them. Modi also wants to learn from the people and therefore he says that if he fell short of their expectations in any way, they should think that he was not able to learn enough. While congratulating the people of Vadodara, he said that there are no enemies in Politics. Politics has only competition. There lies the strength of democracy. He appeals to all political parties and seeks their cooperation in taking the nation forward.

His ideas and dreams about the twenty first century clearly reflect in his speeches. He says, "My mantra is – everyone's cooperation for everyone's progress (*Sabka Saath Sabka Vikas*).These are not merely the words. This is the DNA of my work culture. The people of India have delivered their verdict. We have to take India on to the path of progress. We have to fulfil the dreams of 125 crores Indians." Modi also makes light hearted fun of UPA Government's promises and says, "Our ears are tired of hearing about 21st century being mentioned so often by them. Does anyone have any vision of how to take the country into 21st century?"

He said, "If anyone had the vision and means to take the country into the new millennium, we would not have been in the mess that we are now." Modi regrets the mood of despondency and declares, "I have not given up." He says, "I am surprised to see that we have no friends left in our neighbourhood." While discussing about raising in Foreign Direct Investment in the area of Defence, he says, "The country spends more money on defence equipments and arms than it does on import of Petroleum products. Don't we have engineers who can manufacture these equipments? I notice that in our Engineering Colleges, there is no subject called Defence Engineering."

Modi provides a justified logic in his speeches that the economic structure of the nation can be salvaged from the current dilapidated stage. Tough decisions have to be made in Politics. He also talks of five deficits which if taken care of can ensure progress of the nation. They are fiscal deficit, governance deficit, trust deficit, security deficit and moral deficit. If these can be reinstated, people's morale will get a tremendous boost. Modi asks as to why India was called the golden goose? Why is it that foreigners frequently invaded this country? The reason is that this nation was wealthy and prosperous for many centuries. During our years of slavery, we lost most of our wealth and in the 21st century also we have lost many historic opportunities. We have the capability and strength to record the fastest development growth rate because we have democracy, large skilled manpower and market demand. Many countries do not have these advantages. In the very early years of 21st century, during the regime of Atal ji, we had earned a place for ourselves in BRICKS countries but the later ten years were wasted and we got isolated having missed the bus. Now, we have the challenge of progressing again towards being a superpower.

Taking a serious note of the current worrisome and pathetic state of economy, Modi rues that it is not only the danger of current deficit account which haunts the nation but we are also faced with the dangers of moral deficit, governance deficit, trust deficit and security deficit. It is our strength that if we have the faith, we can still make progress. But our faith is in shambles today. If only we lack some things, they are direction, commitment and dedication. Who will ensure these?

While throwing up the challenge of starting the mass movement towards progress, he says that Mahatma Gandhi started the mass movement to get freedom; today a similar movement is necessary to achieve progress. It will not be achieved by making a policy but it should be reinforced through good governance and credibility. When the country is passing through tough time, we must do some fundamental introspection.

For the youth and the citizens to lead a life of respect and pride, for qualitative improvement in standard of living, why should we not dream of respectable jobs for everyone? To abolish the wide gap between the poor and the rich and to eradicate the inconsistencies between rural and urban India is the dire need of this hour. We will have to give priority to areas like health and education by making qualitative improvements and transformation in these fields. Modi says that for the balanced growth of the nation's economy, we must utilize manufacturing, industry, agriculture and service sectors with appropriate balanced emphasis. Investment should be made not only in industry but also in infrastructural areas like agriculture, water resources, power and roads. It is necessary to spread a sense of progress in these areas. To lay emphasis on infrastructure and research is the need of the hour. Modi has been giving valuable inputs from time to time for the balanced growth of the nation through all states by having flexible policies and strategies so that all sections of society and all segments of trade and commerce can surge ahead with zeal.

Narendra Modi has been nurturing these thoughts for twenty first century not only from today but ever since he became the Chief Minister of Gujarat for the first time. He has always been emphatic that if the responsibility he has been given is carried out diligently then people are bound to be benefitted. People generally try to run away from responsibilities but he delivered his responsibilities exceptionally well. This is the reason that after he was elected for the first time, the voters in Gujarat had no other thought other than making him the Chief Minister again. Now that he has become the Prime Minister of India, we have to see how many more times voters in India will prefer to re-elect him.

Journey to Prime Ministership

BJP had already won half the battle by nominating Modi as the Prime Ministerial candidate because his candidature passed the very test which the voters expected him to. He was successful in convincing voters from every sect, religion and region that he was the only one who could fulfil the dream of a prosperous 21st century for India through his agenda for progress, through his departure from sectorial politics, rock-solid leadership and result orientation. This was the reason why BJP got support from every nook and corner of the country. The support might have been of varying degree and proportion but they got the support in one form or the other.

All parties including Congress kept reiterating about secularism but contrary to this, Modi won the confidence and caught the imagination of young voters by speaking about employment, progress of the nation, infrastructure growth, eradication of corruption and many similar serious issues which touched their lives. He made it clear to the voters that the opposition parties were misguiding them by alternatively talking about poverty eradication or saving the secular fabric of India thus running away from the real issues facing the nation. BJP had taken the right decision regarding the poll alliances. In 2004, BJP had lost the elections because they sought alliance from Trinamul Congress, Telugu Desam Party, JDU, Shiv Sena, Akali Dal and AIDMK and some more which made them repent at a later stage. The number of candidates from BJP had dropped considerably. They learnt a lesson from this and collaborated with 24 parties and under the leadership of Modi, restructured the National Democratic Alliance. Modi did not compromise on the issue of his being the leader and he side-tracked old ally like JDU in Bihar. Accepting the logic behind local leadership, he also bid farewell to Assam Gan Parishad in Assam. The direction in which the wind blew was clear from the day when Ram Bilas Paswan who had parted company in Atal Bihari's government returned in the fold of restructured NDA. Apart from this, to deflate the egos of Nitish Kumar and Lalu Prasad in Bihar, BJP took Upendra Kushawaha's Bharatiya Lok Samata Party into confidence. In UP, they took a new party like 'Apna Dal' into its fold. In Maharashtra, they took the support of Ramdas Athawale and Raju Shetty's parties apart from the old ally like Shiv Sena. Joining hands with Raj Thakare's Maharashtra Navnirman Sena was a golden opportunity. They also had the old ally Akali Dal in Punjab and Janahit Congress in Haryana as their supporters.

Party adopted aggressive campaigning as their strategy. Right from the first day, one could witness all the methods like social networking, rallies and ground level contact supplemented by booth management being practised. BJP was seen as a party with a strong determination to win the elections. Modi was seen bitterly attacking the mismanagement of Congress government. Time and again the campaign made 'Development and progress' as its pivotal agenda and people were taken into confidence by emphasizing about the success of BJP governed states and Atal government's achievements. During the campaign both traditional and modern methods were simultaneously adopted and Modi took part in 5,827 rallies. BJP proclaimed that they had carried out the biggest exercise in public contact in the entire history of elections held so far in India. During these campaigns and rallies held from 15th Sept, 2013 to 10th May, 2014, Modi addressed 437 public meetings in 25 states and participated in 1350 3D rallies. It is reported that Modi was a part of 5,827 meetings which also include 4000 of his 'Chai par charcha' (discussion over a cup of tea) programmes. In this programme, he had discussed with large population of people in many cities through video link medium. Apart from this, one may also note the two mammoth rallies which he held in Vadodara and Varanasi. He had contested from these two constituencies.

Even before the election dates were announced, to create the election fever and euphoria, he addressed 38 rallies in 21 states. The first rally which was held as a part of this initiative was in Udhampur on 26th March, 2014 which he named as 'Bharat Vijay Rally' (India Victory Rally). As a part of this mass initiative, he held 196 rallies in 25 states and travelled all over the country over a distance of more than 2 lakh km.

BJP claims that the election campaign conducted by it is nothing less than historic and unique. Party claims that this campaign spearheaded by Modi, is one of the biggest public awakening initiative in the history. Having realised the importance of UP, he held the most number of rallies there. Modi wave was already sweeping the nation but to support it, there was a need to select the right candidates. BJP fielded every big name. For example, in Uttarakhand, they fielded three past CMs including B. C. Khanduri, Bhagat Singh Koshyari and Ramesh Pokhriyal. In the same manner, in UP, it fielded veteran stalwarts like Rajnath Singh, Kalraj Mishra, Murali Manohar Joshi and Santosh Gangwar. In addition to this, it gave tickets to new but imposing distinguished professionals and public figures like Gen.V K Singh and Satyapal Singh. They accepted the challenge thrown in by Aam Aadmi Party in Delhi and fielded new faces like Mahesh Giri and seasoned veterans like Dr Harshvardhan.Wherever BJP was already in power, it got thumping success. BJP had a clean sweep in states like Rajasthan, MP, Chhattisgarh, and Gujarat.

When Mani Shankar Iyer cynically commented on Modi that he should sell tea outside Congress party's office, Modi smartly converted it into an election issue and started his 'Chai par Charcha' as a campaign initiative. He proudly called himself as a son of a poor and challenged the princely Rahul Gandhi. When Priyanka branded him as a low level politician indulging in pedestrian politics, he brandished his OBC card which flourished and made her to bite her own words. When his opponents tried to intimidate him by talking of Muslim votes and by mentioning Secularism, Modi held the bull by its horn and made all their allegations defunct.

The people of India were seething with anger after having suffered under the Congress government for 10 years. The stench of 2G scandal and Coalgate during UPA's second tenure has nauseated the common man and filled his mind with venom about the misdeeds of Congress. Very bad economic conditions, lack-lustre and uninspiring leadership of Rahul Gandhi also helped BJP in building public opinion against Congress. BJP could successfully instil the confidence in the minds of voters that only they could provide them relief from the misdeeds of Congress and if they wasted their precious votes by casting them in favour of regional parties, then Congress could come back to power and grab it.

With this background, the relentless efforts of Modi bore fruits. He tirelessly went around campaigning for his party. His team sent a singular message, be it on a social networking site or booth management. They wanted voters to cast their votes to Modi and not regional candidates. 'Ab ki bar Modi Sarkar' (This time, Modi government), became a nationwide slogan and now it has turned into a reality. If you listen carefully you will hear the name Modi-Modi reverberating in air and whenever there was this roar, Modi spoke to 125 crores of his countrymen and shared his dream with them, then it became easy to occupy the seat of a Prime Minister was even easier.

The uniqueness of Modi's personality is that wherever he has served, he has done it with full devotion and he has always tried to accomplish everything he wanted through fair means. When he associated himself with Sangh in 1972, he served the institution with complete devotion. He kept spreading the message wherever he was sent as a propagator. After he moved from RSS to BJP, he took charge as a party worker and delivered his duties with dedication and sincerety.

Even today, he proudly admits that he is not bigger than BJP. When the results of 2007 Legislative Assembly polls were announced and in the MLA's meeting of the Modi said very modestly that people, who say that Modi is bigger than the Party, are unaware of the history and tradition of BJP and JanaSangh. A son can never be greater than his mother. He became emotional and said in no uncertain terms that it is an indication of mental aberration to think that Modi is bigger than Party. Modi said that during the days of JanaSangh, many party candidates lost their deposits in most of the polls. During those days, many dedicated party workers and their families served the party selflessly. Referring to his own profile, he says that people find his profile awe-inspiring and big because their own vision and outlook are small and limited. It stops there. If we exemplify your focus then you will be able to see thousands of party activists who have supported me and carried me all along. This viewpoint is really worthy of praise because unless one changes his way of thinking, you will have only one outlook.

Modi always associated struggle with the aim of his life as an integral part and therefore he always keeps thinking of struggle. During his tenure, when one looks at the kind of problems he faced and studies how he firmly won over them, one realises that in the same process he talked of rights of people too. This right may be social or legal. It may be the right of a farmer or it may pertain to an agitation by the farmers, Modi has always worked with dedication and transparency keeping the cause of peoples' rights on the top of his mind. His personality had and will always have struggle as an integral part.

It is very common to see that lot many people are always him Chief Ministers and even with the politicians also and not only to this, a large group of favour seekers keeps moving around them. Modi is an exception to this. There are only three people, apart from his security staff, who live with him in his bungalow. He has one cook and two attendants with him. Narendra Modi has no inclination to have large number of people around him and holding court. Even he has not allowed his two attendents, Mr O.P Singh & Tanmay to come to his house.

Even those who are not agreed with Modi, use to appreciate his working style. He use to work from 8AM to 11PM and he is also successful in showing that he is an honest person. He wants to keep doing his work all time and use to advise to the nearby people to work because without doing any work, nothing could be happened.

Most people only think that Narendra Modi is only a politician but the fact is that he is not only a politician. Had he not been a politician, he would have surely become a wonderful poet and author. The thoughts expressed by him in his literary works are rarely seen in other authors'. People may wonder where does he find time to write. Yes, he writes and he has authored more than a dozen such books which were famous and discussed. People do read his Gujarati poems even today and want to continue to read. Although, he finds less time to write but whatever he wrote, that was discussed a lot.

When Modi joined RSS in 1972, immediately after a few years, emergency was imposed in the country. In those days, after he went underground, he saw the conditions during emergency from very close quarters and he tried to put those scenes in words. His first book in Gujarati was 'Sangharshama Gujarat' and it received all round praise. The same book was published in Hindi too, (Aapaatakal mein Gujarat). Apart from this, his major works include 'Shree Guruji Ek Swayamsewak', 'Yatharth dharma', and 'Patro mein Guruji'. His recent work, 'Jyotipunj' was discussed widely. This book was published after he became Chief Minister for the third time. This book consists of his philosophical image.

Modi has to write more and this is not his last work. This is only a glimpse but his readers and well-wishers are hoping that he will write continuously and will make the world to become aware of his thoughts. People talk about his poems too. Whenever he finds time, the poet in him comes out to express himself. His format of expression may be prose or poetry. Even today, when he has an opportunity be with intellectuals and literature lovers, he takes the opportunity to recite his poems to them.

There are many aspects of his life which are only known to him and nobody knows that, but whatever has come out about his qualities of his life, has resulted into many other fascinating facets of his personality. In order to satiate his curiosity and to enhance his knowledge, he has travelled to many countries and learnt from those visits. Modi has visited almost two dozen countries which include Australia, Japan, Singapore, Switzerland, and Britain and during each of his visits, he has made it a point to benchmark the development models of those countries.

When he went to Russia along with Atal Bihari Vajpeyee when he was PM, he studied many development models to be implemented for the progress of Gujarat, He also discussed about them with Vajpayee. He said to Vajpayee that if we adopt some of the development models of Russia, our country too could progress. Unfortunately, Vajpayee was unable to understand that model but Modi understood that and experimented with it in Gujarat. When he saw some more models of progress of other countries, he tried to show them in Gujarat also. Today, the people of India is expecting that he will take India on the path of progress like other developed nations.

A Struggleful Life

Narendra Modi was born in a small village, Vadnagar, in Mehasana district of North Gujarat in September 1950. He was brought up in such surroundings where the values like charity, service and social indebtedness got imbibed in him in a very natural way. In the sixties, in spite of being very small, he voluntarily served the soldiers who were passing through the railway station to fight the Indo-Pak war. In 1967, he served the flood affected families from Gujarat. By the virtue of his inner qualities like excellent organizing capabilities and deep understanding of human psychology, he lent his services to Akhil Bharatiya Vidyarthi Parishad (All India Students Federation), ABVP. He also made valuable contribution to many socio- political agitations in Gujarat.

He had to face many difficulties and problems from his very young days but he accepted every challenge and changed that into an opportunity to prove his mettle through his strong personality and courage. Especially when he took admission in college and University to acquire higher education, his path was full with struggles and painful hard work, but he remained strong and undeterred like a true warrior and soldier in the battle of his life. He never accepted defeat or failure. With the same grit and determination, he finished his post-graduate studies in Political Science. He joined the Rashtriya Swayamsewak Sangh (RSS), an organization which had devoted itself to the social and cultural development of India and thus imbibed the qualities of selfless service, social responsibility and fierce national pride.

During his tenure in RSS, he participated in the anti-Corruption mass Agitation to protest against corruption called 'Nav Nirman

Andolan' and the agitation during the 19 long months of Emergency (June 1975 to January 1977) when the basic rights of the Indian Citizens were strangulated. He carried out very important roles during these agitations. He was underground during this entire period and he secretly participated in the agitation against the oppressive and strangulating regime of the Central Government with great fervour thus keeping the spirit of democracy alive.

He joined Bharatiya Janata Party (BJP) in 1987 thus entering into mainstream Politics. Within a year, he was nominated as the Organising Secretary of the Gujarat Unit of the party. By then he had earned a name as a very capable organiser. He took up the challenge to rejuvenate and activate the party workers in the true sense which started immensely benefitting the party. When an alliance Government was formed at the Centre in 1990, the alliance lasted for only very few months. However in 1995 elections, BJP won two third majority majorities on its strength alone, it was successful to form the government and came to power. The rein of Gujarat is in the hands of BJP ever since.

He established his identity as a skilful and able strategist during 1988 to 1995 which helped the Gujarat BJP to do the groundwork with great success to form government. During this period, he was given the responsibility of organising two major national level events. One was the long Rath Yatra (Chariot rally) from Somnath to Ayodhya by Lalkrishna Advani and the second was Yatra (rally) from Kanyakumari situated on the southernmost tip to Kashmir. The credit of BJP's rise to power in New Delhi in 1998 is given to these two very successful events in which Modi's contribution was very valuable.

He was nominated as the National Secretary of the party in 1995 and he was also given the responsibility of five major states which was a matter of great achievement for any youth leader. He was promoted to the post of General Secretary (Organization) in 1998. Till October 2001, when he became the Chief Minister of the most prosperous and progressive state in India, he kept rendering his service as the General Secretary to the party. During his tenure at the national level, he was given the responsibility of looking after sensitive states like Jammu & Kashmir in addition to the regional units of many important states. He also emerged as an important spokesman of the party during the same period and he also played a major contributing role on many critical occasions.

During this period, he travelled to many countries and held discussions with many distinguished leaders. These experiences not only gave him a global outlook but it also reinforced his strong resolve to serve the nation and thus help

India establishes herself as a socio- economic power. Modi has always been inquisitive and curious and wants continue to be so. It is in his genes to keep making new experiments. He accepts new experiments with a sense of personal challenge and purpose and he goes after them relentlessly to make them successful. He has deep interest in new developments in Science and Technology.Threfore, during his travels, he is always in search of what is new and asserts that till an individual discovers and does something new all the time, there is use of his being a mere visitor nor will he develop a habit of being innovative. That is the reason he has always made efforts to conduct new experiments. He has always considered creative and effective use of time as an imporatnat personal trait. Curiosity is such an important part of his persona that if he comes to know that a personal task cannot be accomplished, and then he would rather evolve a formula to do it than take a fatalistic stand. People close to him know that he does not have 'no' in his dictionary. He would rather look for the solution to convert this 'no' into a 'yes'. He always tries to understand the reason for 'no' and then search for its solution. With this curious disposition, he has been observed to have introspected along with inventors and thinkers. When he has to embark on something new, he prepares a strategy; a strategy which is helpful for the progress of the society and nation. Today, if he is called as 'Vikas Purush' (Man of development and progress) it is not difficult to understand the reason because his thinking starts with progress and ends with progress.

He was asked to take the reins of Gujarat in his hands in October 2001 by the party. He took the oath on 7th October, 2001 when Gujarat was passing through a very difficult phase as an outcome of the mammoth calamity of earthquake in 2001 and its aftermath and many similar calamities. This skilled strategist decided to take up the task of rejuvenation making use of all his national and international experience with enthusiasm.

He was confronted with the major challenge of re-establishment and rehabilitation the earthquake affected regions. Bhuj had become a city of garbage and waste and thousands of people were put in makeshift pathetic shelters. Bhuj today is a standing example of how he fought with the adverse conditions, won over them and transformed the city with all round progress.

Even when the work of rehabilitation and reestablishment was going on, he had not lost sight of introspection and churning in the border context. Gujarat has always concentrated on Industrial growth. Modi concentrated on social issues, decided to remove the anomalies and imbalances in a constructive way so that there can be overall social and economic growth. To do this, he formulated a five point strategy called Panchamrit Yojana for the multifaceted development of the state.

We can see path breaking transformations in the fields of Education, Agriculture and Health; he formulated a clear vision for the future of the state and started development programmes. He restructured the organisational structure of the state and put Gujarat on a path of prosperity. Within a span of 100 days after he took over the state, one could clearly see his ambitions and capabilities. With his administrative comprehension, clear vision and integrity of character, he earned huge success in the general elections held in December 2002 and Modi won 128 seats out of 182. In the 2007 elections also, BJP, under the leadership of Modi won a clear majority.

Modi had completed 4000 days of his service to the people of Gujarat on 17th September, 2012. He won the heart and support of people of Gujarat in three consecutive elections. After winming in 2002 and 2007 elections, and also in 2012, BJP, under the leadership of Modi gained a major victory. BJP won 115 seats and he was sworn in as the Chief Minister for the fourth consecutive time. Citizens of the nation wanted to see him as the Prime Minister of the nation in the 2014 elections and therefore BJP got a thumping majority making him the Prime Minister of the country.

Modi during Emergency

Modi has seen the turmoil during the period of Emergency from very close quarters. When he joined RSS as a volunteer and a canvasser in 1972, the country was passing through different kind of political climate. People were fed up with Congress rule. The leadership of Prime Minister Indira Gandhi was not liked by anyone. There were voices of dissent. People were tired of Congress administration. There was an air of protest and agitation all over the country but nobody could imagine in their wildest dreams that 'Emergency' could be imposed in the country. Ultimately, something which was never expected happened. Emergency was declared in the country on 26th June, 1975. This was accompanied by wide-spread protests. Gujarat also had announced a two day strike as a protest. Modi was also aware of the perils of Emergency because he was active in Sangh at that time.

Narendra Modi was in the Gujarat office of the Sangh. The news of imposition of Emergency spread like a wild fire. News like, "JP is arrested Police are on the lookout for Nanaji and Morarji too is arrested. The Sangh office is surrounded by Police. There are raids on the state headquarters of various political parties. Police are patrolling on the streets of Delhi and in many places the army vehicles are also being seen. All contacts with Newspaper offices has been lost. In some offices, Police staff is receiving call" were making rounds. What was happening was beyond comprehension. The activists and party workers of Sangh swung into action. Modi has understood the criticality of the situation and he was ready to take active part in the struggle to oppose Emergency along with his colleagues. The Sangharsh Samiti (Agitation Committee) had organized an emergency meeting. Directives were given that 26th and 27th June be announced as days of protest in Gujarat. It was decided to organize public meetings, as far as possible, in all towns and cities on 26th to protest against imposition of Emergency. A mammoth rally was organised in Vadodara on 28th to protest against Emergency. After this, the chain of protests and opposition did not stop till the end of Emergency.

People who opposed Emergency were being arrested. Everyone has gone underground. Narendra Modi was also fighting against this oppressive imposition in the capacity of a trusted soldier of the party. He was constantly in touch with his colleagues. His alertness and activeness can be judged from the fact that he was able to gather all the news and information through his network of underground intelligence. He used to communicate the plight of his collegues to the masses. Makarand Desai, in his letter dated 16th July, 1976, said regarding Modi that through the medium of his letters he got all the information and his network and arrangement were praiseworthy. He was able to get all the information from there. BBC also included the same information in its broadcasts. Therefore it was important that the information should be promptly available. He continued to send information to people abroad who were also involved in the struggle against Emergency. This helped in spreading the information all over the world about what was happening in India. As soon as he received a letter from Makarandbhai, he would promptly reply it so that he knew what was really happening in India. In one of his letters Makarandbhai says, "Brother Narendra, I was very happy to receive your letter. Please continue to write so that we can carry out our mission easily. Please keep sending us important informations and news which is relevant to our struggle. Please send us all the news that specifically pertains to failure of Emergency so that we can publish it in our newspaper, 'Satya wani', so that the whole world comes to know about it.

He received similar letters from New York and Nairobi and he also replied them in all thoroughness and sincerity so that he could gather support of people abroad in his struggle against Emergency. In India, the conditions created by Emergency were deplorable and were deteriorating day by day. People opposing Emergency were en-masse sent to jails but the method of opposing Emergency which was adopted by Narendra Modi and similar leaders could be called unique because they were telling people living abroad about the conditions prevailing within and the turmoil India was going through. They were sending news about the dictatorship and the oppressive measures with scant respect for democracy. The mental status and the tale of this struggle can be seen in his first book, 'Sangharshama Gujarat'. When the struggle against Emergency was started people made fun of it in many ways. Modi writes that he was in touch with many sections of the society during his 'underground agitation'. In the beginning, people looked at the agitation with sarcasm. In an attempt to make fun of us, they used to sing praises of 'Bahenji's bravery but as people started realising the seriousness of the issue, people and society's expectations from us went on increasing. People who were sarcastic could not afford to be same anymore. Modi continuously fought in this war like a soldier. All along he was engaged in making the information reach the people as well as gathering news from his countrymen. With his dedication to the cause, he used to receive information not only from India but from abroad and he too sent information from Gujarat. There are many events from Emergency which he had narrated in his own words.

Modi narrates, "By the end of 1975, many meetings were arranged in Gujarat and therefore, most of the leaders were present in Gujarat itself. I was to go and meet Ravindra Verma on morning of 1st January, 1976. He was waiting for me in the house of Ramlal Parikh. As soon as I met him, I wished him 'Happy new year' and greeted him. Verma ji replied and said, "Narendra ji, I was about to wish you a happy new year as soon as I saw you but you are follower of Hindutva (Hindutva wadi) and therefore I thought that you may take offence and therefore I did not wish you. But you ...!" After this Modi responded to Verma ji that it is the greatness of Hindu religion that it does not allow people walking on its path to become narrow-minded.

This episode reflects well on Modi's psyche. What he said during the days of Emergency still continues to help him to continue to progress, maintain his self-respect which is because of the strength he has got by following Hindutva. He was successful to leave his imprint during the days of Emergency because of his personality. Otherwise it was a period of turmoil where many fighters like him struggled equally hard but only Modi could succeed in his struggle, came out with dignity and today the population of Gujarat is feeling proud of him.

Pride of Gujarat

Modi and Gujarat are synonymous. Gujarat was in the news all over the world during the 2002 Godhra tragedy. It is futile to go into the details of the pain of Godhra but Narendra Modi brought a revolution in Gujarat which nobody else in the past had been able to. During the Parliamentary Elections, the entire nation looked at him with abated breath. It was secondary that which party would win the elections as compared with the question if Narendra Modi would win. Narendra Modi's win was discussed more than the win of BJP. Every voter in the country was guessing about him while Modi had no such doubt in his mind. He was going ahead enthusiastically with his agenda of progress and frankly, which other agenda stood a chance to win. He was not asking for votes as an individual but he was seeking the voters' confidence for the agenda of progress. On one hand he was seen as a representative of Hindutva while on the other he personified the glory of progress. Who should be elected was a million dollar question.

It will not be an exaggeration if Modi is called the pride of Gujarat. No Chief Minister has done as much as compared with what he has done for Gujarat. In May 1960, Jeevaraj Mehta became the first Chief Minister of Gujarat under the banner of Indian National Congress. After that, for many years, Congress continued to rule Gujarat. Many stalwarts like Balwantrai Mehta. Hitendrabhai Desai, Ghanashyambhai Ojha, Chimanbhai Patel, Madhavsingh Solanki and Amarsingh Solanki became the Chief Minister under the patronage of Congress but no Chief Minister could claim progress of the state. As a matter of fact Keshubhai Patel and Sureshchandra Mehta also became the Chief Ministers under

BJP rule. The state was under President's Rule on five occasions. Apart from this, Babubhai Patel became the Chief Minister in 1975 as a Janata Front candidate. Janata Party, Janata Dal also formed Governments in the state but the only man who was credited with progress and credited with the title of 'Vikas Purush' is Narendra Modi. What makes him worthy of this title? What is it that others lack to earn this title? There must have been something in him which gave him this credit. Some knew him as the spokesman of Hindutva but the real Modi was known only to those who got the benefit of roads, water and means of transportation in their villages and towns.

His opponents defy him by claiming that all this talk of progressive Gujarat is mere slogan mongering by Modi. How true is this allegation? Yes, Modi does talk of progress all along but not the way the opponents do as a matter of ritual. I might have not witnessed one hundred percent progress in the regions which I visited but I could see the beginning of the efforts bearing fruits. I saw a different dimension of progress when compared with the states which invite you to see progress. Democracy must encourage critics. Narendra Modi gave priority to critics and worked in a manner commensurate with it. The more opposition he got, harder he worked. Even before the Legislative Assembly elections, one could see the Modi antagonists were agitating against him from Delhi to Ahmedabad alleging that Modi's claims were false. They claimed that the farmers were committing suicide without substantiating the claims. They claimed that their inability to pay the loans borrowed from the Government. They did not have any proof. All they wanted to do was to plant allegations so that he could be pushed back. It did not matter if they had to make false claims by uttering blatant lies for defaming him. The general population of Gujarat were looking for peace and prosperity through progress. The opponents claimed that Muslims opposed him. This was not so. In fact they were with him because they felt safe with Modi. The opponents felt that Godhra tragedy would alienate Modi from the entire population of Gujarat. But this was not so. The tragedy of Godhra is bound to keep haunting Gujarat for many centuries but it is also a fact that the screams of passengers who were burnt alive in Sabarmati Express were also silenced.

However, despite these deplorable blots in his regime, it is not easy for the people of Gujarat to ignore the visionary in Modi. Those who have seen the performance of Chief Ministers since 1960 till Modi became Chief Minister will surely see the difference. His motto of progress is in glorious contrast with the performance of the yesteryears' Chief Ministers. Progress has become an integral part now and will continue irrespective of Modi. Gujarat is now being identified with progress and will continue to be known for it. People working with him say that he is not only a politician but a visionary too. He thinks differently when compared with other political leaders. He has a different and unique outlook in everything he does.

Which regime do you prefer between the long years of rule of Congress, a few years of BJP and then Modi's governance? There were long debates on this issue. When Modi took over the leadership of Gujarat, it was passing through a difficult phase and progress was the only answer to it. The entire region was struggling as an aftermath of the disastrous calamity of an earthquake in Bhuj. The rehabilitation and rejuvenation of the people were a difficult challenge. Modi took up the challenge and provided such an arrangement to the temporarily housed victims through housing and jobs that it has resulted in development of the entire region of Bhuj. Modi had seen a dream where the people had accepted the challenge but they did not have the means to fight it. He had the strength of power. The investors had the power of money. Why should it not be used? He took it up as a challenge and prepared the blue-print for progress and slowly started to implement it. Result; work for the people and their faith in him.

His first priority was the development of the towns and villages of Gujarat. He was of the opinion that when the towns developed, the district too would develop and when the district developed the region is bound to develop. He started Samaras Gram Yojana, Gram Sabha, Teerth Gram Yojana, Jyoti Gram Yojana, Gokul Gram Yojana, Vishwa Gram Yojana, Shramyogi Yojana with this resolve and started to give them a concrete shape. His purpose was to start something unique on this land of Mahatma Gandhi and only then would his dream of the progress of Gujarat be fulfilled. Among the people who call him the pride of Gujarat also include the Gujaratis who are spreaded all over the world and who want to contribute to Gujarat. When they see the style of Modi's working they have more faith in him than their own selves.

Businessmen and professionals from Gujarat are spread all over the world today. Some continue to be associated with Gujarat while some have broken their bonds with Gujarat but they too want to do something for Gujarat as a matter of pride and self-respect for Gujarat. They nurtured this dream in the past too but there was no outlet to their wish. People who ruled Gujarat before Modi did everything with a selfish motto. They did everything to promote their friends and relatives but nothing for Gujarat.

When Modi became the Chief Minister, he dreamt big. He wanted to give his best for Gujarat. Everyone supported his thoughts. People who did not want to support came forward later when they saw his resolve. They came forward and promised him their support. They told, " Modi Ji we are with you." Irrespective of which part of the globe they lived in; be it Britain, Europe or USA, every Gujarati told him that they wanted to join him in his journey and in his struggle. Modi respected everyone's feelings. He made a strategy by taking along everyone with him so that progress and development could be achieved. He never thought that if he borrowed someone's idea, it would not match his stature but he believed that if he worked on the idea, made it worthy of implementation, he might achieve success. This was his viewpoint. He accepted all the ideas with open arms and with a smile, irrespective of their origin. He listened to everyone carefully. He learnt from everyone. It did not matter if he was a farmer or a petty shop-owner, a worker or an officer. He treated everyone with respect and tried to know from him what development meant to him. He tried to understand how they could move forward together. Only when this was achieved, his efforts for development bore fruits and with this resolve to see a developed Gujarat, he also spread the message that Gujarat has to be developed, not the development of single man. When it was a matter of Gujarat, then all the Gujaratis, spread all over the globe, put their hands together and become one. Some people did oppose but it was like a minor dissent within a family. This was the case with Gujarat too but Modi made sure that he took along everyone with him. He never showed his disappointment towards people who were not willing to join him but he wanted to know his reasons, thoughts and solutions too. He welcomed everyone and made a promise that their ideas would bear fruits.

Today, we can see Modi's determination is fulfilling. He is now being seen as the pride and symbol of Gujarat. After being sworn in as the Prime Minister recently, every citizen is looking at him with the hope that he would open a new chapter of progress in the history of the Nation after Gujarat.

Modi in Pictures

Narendra Modi in NCC uniform

Narendra Modi as a symbol of youth power

Narendra Modi as a skilled orator who can keep his audience spell bound

BJP President Rajnath Singh is also an admirer of Modi

His admirers include people from all walks of life

Narendra Modi's encouragement helps the chess players of Gujarat earn a place in Guinness Book

His beloved mother feeds him sweets to celebrate his win in the Parliamentary elections

He pays his respect to the Father of the nation on Rajghat before taking an oath as a Prime Minister

Welcoming the Prime Minister of Pakistan Nawaz Sherif at the swearing in ceremony

President of India Pranab Mukherjee administering the oath of secrecy to the new Prime Minister Narendra Modi

Greeting the people after becoming Prime Minister

First day in the office as a Prime Minister

People from all over the world listened to his thoughts in India Today conclave

With Yoga Guru and spiritual saint Baba Ramdev in Haridwar

Ratan Tata and Chief Minister Narendra Modi with the ambitious Nano car

The responsibility of resolving the complex relationship issues rests on the shoulders of both the Prime Ministers

Modi and controversies

Modi and controversies are inseparable. They go hand in hand. However, Modi has not been controversial on personal grounds at any time but there is something in him which keeps him entrenched in controversy at all times. Starting from development projects in his region, his every act is always shrouded in controversy. There cannot be a bigger controversy than the way in which he was projected in Godhra tragedy. He was summarily accused and held responsible for Gujarat riots. Allegations were hurled at him and he faced stiff opposition all around. Media also started accusing and making direct allegations against him as if he was personally responsible and the entire chain of events was his charade.

The riots of 2002 in Gujarat which happened during his regime killed at least two thousand people belonging to minorities. Riots broke out when Sabarmati Express coming from Ayodhya, in which volunteers (karsewak) were also coming, caught fire and 58 volunteers were charred to death. As an aftermath of this, Modi's figure emerged as a staunch Hindutva supporting leader. Media even crowned him with the title 'Hindu Hriday Samrat' and as a result he became a hero for those people who strongly believed in Modi's staunch Hindutva supporting philosophy. The speed, at which Modi was slandered and criticized, at the same time his political image also grew up among those who has accepted him. Sometimes his remarks on Afzal Guru or Sohrabudin were criticized but this only helped in making his image very strong as a fanatic.

If we start looking at the controversies where he has been involved in starting from the Godhra riots of 2002, you will observe that he was projected not only at national level but at international level too. The riots echoed right before Gujarat elections when the investigations made by Tehelka revived its memories and truth came to light. What is the truth? Even today the question remains unanswered but the way Tehelka came out with an expose, even after five years after it, Gujarat massacre continues to be a burning issue. Many versions by State Government, Police, victims of riots and civil right activists have come out with many versions which have been a subject of bitter debate. The revolutionary and shocking investigations by Tehelka brought forth the shameful truth behind the massacre from the lips of the same people who were responsible for this gory act.

Tehelka took six months to logically put together the chronology of the entire episode. What was Godhra massacre and what were the controversial remarks of Modi? Why were fingers of doubt being pointed out at Modi? What is the status of this incident even after 4 years?

The manner in which Tehelka has investigated the riots and held Modi responsible, it exposes an entirely different aspect of his personality but the law is unable to understand and accept this truth. If this was true, why he was not punished. In spite of this alleged involvement why has he been able to create a place in the hearts of Gujaratis and then what would qualify for being called the truth. This is also a question. Tehelka reports stated in a recorded statement, a BJP member says that he was present in a meeting where CM had given them three days to take revenge. His exact words were that he gave us three days in which we were free to do whatever we wanted. He said that he would not be able to give them any more time. This was his frank and open statement. He ordered them to stop the rampage after three days and all the violence stopped.

According to one of the alleged persons of 'Naroda Patiya Massacre', on the day of massacre Modi came there and thanked everyone and said that everyone there deserved to be complimented. One of the senior VHP activists, travelling in Sabarmati Express, said, 'Muslims have played a one-day-match with us. They have given us a target of 60 and we have to win this match at any cost. Therefore, you must not stop till the runs scored. Modi has allowed us to do as we please. Police was also with us.'

It also became clear during the conversation that bombs were make-ready in the factories of senior activists of Bajrang Dal and VHP. Arms were procured from Uttar Pradesh, Madhya Pradesh and Punjab and they were distributed among many teams under the instructions of senior members of Sangh family.

Ashish Khaitan, who was the undercover reporter of Tehelka, met many conspirers and rioters who voluntarily narrated how they killed many Muslims. One of the BJP members revealed startling facts. He said that bombs and even the rocket launchers used during massacre which were make-ready in his firecracker making unit. Many conspirers have also mentioned about those meetings which were held all over the state on the night of 27th February, 2002. Immediately after the Sabarmati Express fire incident, a plan was prepared in those meetings to aptly retaliate to the Godhra incident. During the investigations, the conspirers and rioters candidly admitted how the Police had collaborated with them and how it was lending a free hand in accomplishing what they had planned. They narrated how the dead bodies were shifted from Naroda Patia to Ahmedabad by the Police Commissioner so that he could report less number of riot victims. Eyewitnesses described how the Police Officers showered bullets.

It also became evident during the investigations how the entire Law and Order machinery was disbanded. A panel of defence lawyer had been constituted beforehand to save the accused. Two Pulic prosecuters lawyers admitted that instead of helping the victims to get justice, they were helping the accused and how they assisted to arrive at a compromise between the alleged and the victims by giving bribes. The chain of breaking the law and order does not stop here. A senior lawyer representing the Government has in fact raised doubts on the integrity of Nanavati Shah Commission. He alleged, 'Shah was favouring us.'

In another important investigation, Tehelka has exposed the utter lie behind the news about the fire in Coach no.-S-6 of Sabarmati Express where it was alleged that it was a pre-planned conspiracy. Many eye witnesses admitted to Tehelka that they had given false testimony due to many reasons. For instance, one of the major witnesses of the Police said that he and his accomplices were given a bribe of Rs 50000 for giving a false statement by the Chief Investigating Officer, Noel Parmar. Two BJP members, who had claimed to be eye witnesses during the Godhra massacre and identified many accused, admitted that they were, in fact, not present on that day at Godhra station. They claimed that they gave false testimony for the benefit of Hindutva.

The findings of investigations made by Tehelka were published just before the elections but all the turbulence and commotions, which it created, got silenced during the elections. Although, this report came into light and Modi was accused as guilty also but the allegations have been a part of him since 2002.

Modi has been under limelight as the accused in Godhra massacre and his name is mired in the controversy but despite this allegation, he has never lost his composure. In fact, he has confronted the truth with firmness and resolve. If he had erred, he would have probably been scared but his silence has always underlined the fact that he is not lying, not erred and has always proven similar allegations to be false.

He faced opposition about his role in Godhra massacre in all possible ways. His effigies were burnt all over the country. He faced bitter controversies. This massacre was discussed in Parliament, on the streets, among intellectuals and at home. People who make the massacre as a point of animated discussion forget that the country has witnessed many similar unfortunate riots and yet, even after so many years, the real culprits have not been identified; Even if we assume for a moment that Narendra Modi is guilty, let the citizens decide that he is so, or is he guilty only because he was the Chief Minister of Gujarat at the time of riots and he could not punish the real culprits to justice.

Narendra Modi has been controversial but what are the reasons behind it? It is not in his nature to get into controversies. When he was invited to address Asian Hotel's Owners in New York, he was not granted the US visa because of his alleged role in the riots. The visa controversy reached to such a level that everyone including the ruling party and the opposition party criticised the US administration. Modi himself said that refusal to grant him a visa by US is an insult to the Constitution of India, Sovereignty of the nation and five crore Gujaratis. With this controversy the diplomatic relationship between India and USA would highlighted. In the end, Modi had to address the conference through satellite link. In this conference at New York, he said that the act of tarnishing the image of mother India by the USA by not granting him visa was bound to hurt the sentiments of Gujaratis. It was natural. He respected their sentiments. When he said that they did not have to express in words, their devotion to the nation, its tradition and rich values and sense of sacrifice, the entire hall reverberated with applause. Modi might not have been able to personally visit New York but he was able to put his thoughts before his Gujarati brethren. There was opposition there too but he did not care.

Similarly, when he went to Europe to attract foreign investment, he had to face protest. He had to face persistent opposition by Muslim factions. There were agitations accompanied by slogan shouting. Just before the elections, Modi was on a hot seat because of Sohrabudin encounter and resultant death. Followed by this he was in limelight because of his controversial statement regarding death sentence of Afzal guru. When Modi justified the Sohrabudin encounter, the Election Commission slapped a notice on him alleging violation of model code of conduct. He retaliated and gave a reply to the Commission that his statement was a reaction to Sonia Gandhi's statement which called him 'Messenger of death' and therefore his remark should not be misrepresented. Similarly, during the meeting of National Development Council, he severely criticised the Prime Minister for his '15 point programme for minorities' and said that the proposed Minority Fund is an example of communal budgeting. It would split the country and stop growth. He said that poor and backward exist in all castes and religions. Therefore if the Government wants to follow the policy of secularism, if it wants welfare of all the sections then they should not waste national resources in this manner.

Modi was a subject of another controversy when he was shown as Lord Shrikrishna in one of his posters. On the occasion of 50th birthday of the State Energy Minister, Saurabh Patel, he was presented a controversial poster in Bhavnagar. He was shown as Shrikrishna with the Sudarshan Chakra, riding the chariot and Patel was shown as Arjun. BJP's unit President Purushottam Rupala was shown as Yudhishthir and the rivals of BJP were shown as Kauravas led by Keshubhai Patel. Above Modi's picture was the famous verse from Geeta, 'Yada Yada hi dharmasya---'. Modi's opposition had plans to trap him on this issue. He remained undeterred because he knew that he could not get rid of the controversy and therefore he fought it with all his might.

He had to fight many allegations and count allegations during the Parliamentary elections. Opponents pulled out skeletons from the past which they thought could tarnish his image. Modi hardly cared for these and continued his march ahead. He says that he has full faith in God. Time alone will prove what is right and what is wrong. Modi emerged blemishless from all the controversies.

Modi era in BJP

The slogan, 'Ab ki bar, Modi Sarkar' (This time, Modi regime), has become a reality. Modi era has dawned in BJP. In fact, signs of this transformation could be seen when the party decided to fight elections spearheaded by Modi and side-lined Advani. Nobody had the slightest inkling at that time that the Modi era would bring such a massive transformation in the political history of BJP but the Modi's massive win with absolute majority silenced even his staunchest critics.

This is a historic opportunity for him. He has to fulfil the dreams of 'Acche din' of millions of his countrymen. At the same time he has to drive away the fear regarding his image from people's mind which was instilled in their mind by the opposition during the campaign.

The assertion with which he had emphasized his thoughts during the last days of his campaign had almost made sure that a new era was on the threshold. His proclamations had the enthusiasm and teasing which pointed towards change of guard. There have been transformations in BJP from time to time as routine. The first was Atal era, then the Advani era and now Narendra Modi era. After the Balia rally in Uttar Pradesh, he issued a statement to the Media which was something like this-

"Dear Friends,

Today marked the last day of campaigning for the 2014 Parliamentary elections. I concluded the campaign at Balia in East Uttar Pradesh which is also the land of Mangal Pandey, the hero of the 1857 revolution for freedom.

After I was given the responsibility on 13th September, 2013 as a nominee for the post of the Prime Minister, I travelled all over India. My party collegues told me that during this period, I conducted about 5800 campaigns which include 3 D rallies and discussion over tea etc., travelled over a distance of 3 lakh kilometres and addressed 440 rallies and meetings. These also include 'Bharat Victory rallies' which I had started from 26th March, 2014 after seeking blessings from Goddess Maa Vaishno Devi.

One more time, I got this pleasant I opportunity of seeing the diversity of India, people's enthusiasm and different cultures. While serving as a party worker, I already have travelled all over the country but this experience was entirely different, it was absolutely amazing.

I received tremendous love of my people and they gave me their blessings. Generally such a long campaign is said to be very tiresome but on the contrary, I am experiencing a lot of joy now. That experience which is akin to what a devotee feels after a long penance. Through the medium of this campaign, I got an opportunity to seek the blessings of my people who I consider to be my deities. When I look back upon the entire campaign, three words come to mind- extensive, novel and satisfactory!

During our campaign, we tried to convey our agenda of good governance and progress in each corner of our country. People are tired of hearing false promises from those who want to hide corruption. They give the same repeated hollow statements which are based on dynasty rule, which they give to hide their failures. People in this country want a better and brighter future and NDA is the only alliance which can make this transformation.

I was the happiest when I saw the enthusiasm and the tireless efforts of the party activists. It is one thing to witness a rally on TV or on a social media but to work on ground level is an entirely different experience. We do not look at the campaign from the limited view of win or defeat. Election campaign is a memorable experience in the life of the campaign volunteer. This is an opportunity for expansion and strengthening of the organization. This is an opportunity to strengthen the relationship between the public and the organization. Our workers went from door to door and conveyed our message to each individual and we are very proud of them. Our campaign is a story of the hard work of each activist of BJP who has made selfless contribution for the creation of a better India.

During the entire campaign, we have received consistent support and guidance from the senior leadership of the party. We kept deriving enormous strength and inspiration from it and this also added to the enthusiasm of the party workers.

This campaign will also be remembered for its novel experiments. Politics generally means one sided communication but during our 'Discussion over tea' we moved away from the convention and tried a unique experiment. 'Discussion over tea' was held at more than 4000 places all over the country. I sat through these discussions for hours together and listened to their thoughts and different points of views and responded on various issues. I remember one discussion which took place in Wardha in Maharashtra where I met the family of a farmer who had ended his life by committing suicide. I felt very sad. Even after so many years of independence, our farmers feel compelled to end their lives. The present Government was a silent spectator to this and many more similar tragedies. How long can we afford to go on like this?

We also conducted a novel experiment during Bharat Vijay 3D rallies. Within a span of one month, in 12 trips and at 1350 locations I addressed 3 D rallies. Peoples' response and enthusiasm in these 3D rallies was something to be seen to be believed. Many young people complimented me through social media and e mails for visiting their village. People said to our party workers that they want to meet Modi ji on the dais.

For the first time in the election history of India, a special volunteer portal by the name 'India 272' was created. By connecting through this, millions of party workers did many important contributions both on-line and on ground level. I was immensely benefitted by their thoughts and contributions by the way of suggestions. There are immense such possibilities which can enable discussions with well-wishers, accelerate the speed of campaign, give a direction to the contribution of volunteers and in the process, revolutionise campaigning and thus create a paradigm shift.

Social media was also very innovatively used during the campaign. Many friends showed me very creative messages, slogans and infographics on whats app which were very popular. I created my selfie after I voted and also invited others to post their selfies. I held frank discussions with many friends belonging to print and electronic media. Hindi, regional language and English media journalists interviewed me.

I can never forget the love I got during the past eight months. I will always remember the incident at Patna which was rocked with bomb blasts but people's faith in democracy far outweighed this deplorable act. Nobody left the venue and I gave a clear message on that day which I want to repeat even today- we have to decide whether we want to fight with each other or we want to fight together with poverty? The first option will not lead us anywhere whereas the second one will elevate the country to new heights of prosperity and progress.

I want to thank all my countrymen who participated in our rallies, 3D campaigns and discussions in such large numbers. People of all ages, all sections, religions and sects lent their support to us. I have said often that a single Narendra Modi or any other individual cannot single handedly fight elections. The people of India have carried the responsibility on their shoulders. Every citizen of India has become the carrier of the transformation. I conducted many rallies at places where the heat was oppressive and in spite of it, people had come to attend it in large numbers. Some time back I was in Vishkhapatanam where it started to rain suddenly but people did not move. I do not have any words to thank these people. I can only promise to my countrymen that I will repay the debt of their immense love by taking the country on path of unprecedented progress which will become the foundation of a strong India.

The days of campaign are over today but one more round of elections is not yet over. I would like to make an appeal to the people, particularly the youth who have to vote in the last round. Please vote and encourage your friends and relatives to cast their votes. Every vote is important for the nation. During the last days, when I was travelling all over India, I have realized that our country is unique and it also has a responsibility on its shoulders. History is full of instances of the past where our country has shown the path to the entire world from time to time. Once again, now, the need has arisen where it has to play the role of a mentor- A Guru. Let us join our hands together to create a strong and progressive India which will show the path to the entire world."

Sincerely yours
Narendra Modi

These lines, coming from Narendra Modi really impressed millions of voters in the country. Generally, the political leaders resort to maintain a silence after the days of campaign are over and get busy in the guessing game and calculations of how many votes they would get but even after the campaign, Modi continued to be active. He kept getting information about the country from Gandhinagar where he was stationed. It would be interesting to know that even before the election results were announced, he had started discussing the strategy for forming the ministerial cabinet and for the progress of the country along with the officers. It rarely happens that the strategy is ready even before the election is won but Narendra Modi was very confident of his win. He made use of every moment and continued the activity of meeting people and seeking their views. In the entire campaign, the role of established and senior leadership of BJP was very limited. The persons responsible to lead at the Central and State level committees also were trusted lieutenants of Modi, most of whom were considered to be second level leaders. His style of delivering speeches and aggressive manner of campaigning bear ample testimony that this is the victory of newly emerging BJP and all its credit goes to Narendra Modi.

Media and Modi

Major Dailies in Hindi have analysed the historic win of Modi in many different ways. National newspapers published from Delhi like Hindustan, Navbharat Times, Dainik Jagaran, Dainik Bhaskar, Punjab Kesari, Amar Ujala, Rashtriya Sahara etc surely have Modi in their headlines but the presentation of narrating the win is different.

Recently launched newspaper, Navodaya Times has made its front page interesting by putting the photographs of Narendra Modi and Manmohan Singh upside down. The news about Manmohan Singh has the title, No 'NAMO-nishan' of congress (There is no trace of Congress). Accompanying it is the news about Narendra Modi which has the heading 'Solid Sarkar' printed on the top of his photo. It is rare to find such expression and novelty in Hindi journalism. Navoday Times has given a unique heading to each news and made a novel experiment as compared to others. The editorial headlines are also different. They say 'End of family Raj' and beginning of 'Modi Raj'. The editorial says, 'The credit of this unprecedented win may go to anybody but the real reasons are anti-incumbency, peoples' aspirations for progress and Modi wave.'

Navbharat Times has given full credit to Modi in its article '*Abki bar chamatkar*' (Miracle this time). Instead of giving any news on the first page, it has printed just a single remark, 'Chamatkar' which aptly describes the results of sixteenth Parliamentary election's result and no other leader can match the magician performing this trick.

Dainik Jagaran has tried to add punch to the first page by drawing the caricatures of Modi and BJP leaders with the headline 'Ab ki baar Modi Sarkar'. Added to this are the caricatures of the leaders who lost the elections making the contrast all the more interesting and humorous. The editorial titled 'Janata ka Jawab' says that after being ridiculed many times, even at times being insulted too and also being seen as a tyrant by many so called intellectuals from India and abroad, Modi has given an apt answer by winning with a handsome margin.

Amar Ujala has made its front page attractive by printing a large photograph of Modi titled 'Namo-Namo Hindustan'. It remarked on the first page that the people of this nation made him the cynosure of their eyes. The entire nation was swept in the hurricane of 'Namo-Namo' and it destroyed all the equations of caste-creed and religion- regionalism. This historic win of BJP put Congress to finish in many states. The forts of regional stalwarts like Mulayam Singh, Mayawati, Farooq and Nitish Kumar collapsed like nine pins.

Hindustan published a large photograph of Modi with the heading 'Modi ki Mahavijay' (Mega-win of Modi) and published the remarks of its Chief Editor Shashi Shekhar on its front page. Shashi Shekhar writes, 'An unknown entity, born in an obscure village of Gujarat has opened the magical doors and stepped on to Rajpath where every milestone holds a million possibilities and opportunities. History has given him this opportunity and his experienced eyes will be assessing the situation with caution and care. Needless to say that he has enormous opportunities to deliver and they are equally matched with commensurate problems.'

Nai Duniya has published Modi's photograph along with his mother with the heading, 'Acche din aaye' (Good days are here). Its editor Shravan Garg has published his editorial titled 'Virat Daayitwa' on the front page itself . Shravan Garg writes, "Friday, 16th May, 2014 has assumed historic importance. Narendra Modi will be the sculptor of the new destiny of the Indian politics. New Delhi waits for Narendra Modi with abated breath and enthusiasm. It is now final that he will be the next Prime Minister of the nation."

National Duniya has given the statistics of the election along with a large photograph of Modi with the headline, 'Modi Magic'. In his editorial on the first page, Baldevbhai Sharma has written,

“To call the results of 16th Parliamentary elections as historic, incredible or unprecedented sounds hollow when compared with the miracle of Modi. He has crossed all the boundaries of popular political leadership where he stands at a pace where his image as a leader is par comparison.

Dainik Bhaskar has made its front page appealing by printing a tall photograph of Modi and titled it ‘Namo Bharat’. Kalpesh Yagnik’s editorial note is also published along with all relevant statistics. The editorial remarks are published in the form of Questions & Answers. By formulating the questions and answers in an informative way, Modi’s political ambitions have been explained. For instance, the first question asked is, “How did the Modi wave generate?” The answer is, “Modi knew very well that the days were laden with the wave. He knew that his credibility far exceeded everyone else. If not any party, if an individual, a personality or a leader could arouse credibility, the nation was ready to support him.”

Rajasthan Patrika published many interesting facts about Modi’s personality. Some excerpts of the facts published for the readers,

Comb and mirror- close companions-His comb and mirror are his closest aides. He is always very particular about his looks and photographs. He always carries a comb in his pocket. Photographs sent to the press are always scrutinized by him. He has at least half a dozen dresses in his car. He decides what he should wear depends upon his audience.

Didn’t know what he should do when young- He left behind his family in his young days and went to Ramakrishna Mission in Rajkot from where he headed for Belur Math. His next destination was Himalayas. He certainly wanted to do something but was not clear about it. Therefore, he travelled all over India.

He has no ‘best friend’-You may be surprised that he may have millions of well-wishers and fans in the country but he does not have any ‘best friends’. His only best/true friend is his work.

Modi is a copywriter par-excellence: The Parliamentary elections of 2013 presented him as a very effective copy-writer. After this he made such amazing experiments in the General

Elections that the opponents could not match them; rather the opposition ended up ridiculing him. Be it creating catchy slogans or creating a brand, Modi's skills are par excellence. Don't you recall the mobile phones, tea, bread , utensils – you name it- which you had as brand Modi during the elections? This is the effect of brand Modi.

He is a technology buff: Facebook, twitter, blogs, websites, 3D speeches, discussion with tea, live election rally are some of the examples of his passion with technology. As a matter of fact, in closed door meetings too, he prefers multimedia presentations.

He has an eye on every news: At the age of 64, carries on with coordination between technology and his work. He looks at the posters on the net in the morning. He reads each mail and notes. Even when he goes out, he looks at the newspapers and cuttings to know the opinion of his critics.

He got married but did not live with his wife: Narendra Modi got married to Jashodaben but he never lived with her. A couple of days ago, he wrote his wife's name in his nomination paper filed in Gujarat. This generated a lot of controversy. Jashodaben cast her vote also wishing him a glorious win.

He likes to cook: Modi is very conscious about his health. He eats millet roti (bhakari) and khichdi which are cooked in Gujarati style. He can cook also.

He believes in doing by demonstrating: Modi makes a committment to himself and ensures that he meets it. This has been seen many times. After he decided to provide power round the clock in Gujarat, he showed firmness and did something which was almost impossible. He decided to end the problems in providing electricity. He took tough decisions to prevent pilferage of power. He collected overdue bills. His opponents may call him Hitler but the fact is that the power crisis in Gujarat is a thing of the past.

His decisions are based on opportunity and the person: Modi waits for the right time to achieve his targets. He is an expert in identifying the right people in fulfilling his goals and also in removing the people who are inefficient.

Modi likes Saints: During his association with Vishwa Hindu Parishad (VHP), he met a number of saints. He taught 'Gujarati' to sadvi Ritambhara. Her Guru, Swami Parmanand, used to appreciate Modi's knowledge and his thirst for knowledge.

Doors are open for Gujarati Muslims: Contrary to his image, Modi use to meet Gujarati Muslims regularly. In Gandhinagar, it is said that Gujarati Muslims have granted special permission to meet Modi.

He sleeps only for five hours: In his scheme of priorities, work matters more than rest. After he gets up at five or half past five in the morning, generally he carries on his work till 10 in the night. Irrespective of when he goes up to sleep, his waking hour does not change.

His horoscope is similar to Tilak and Bismarck: The astrologers who have seen his horoscope say that Modi who born on 17th September, 1950 has Antardasha of Rahu. This is considered to be auspicious for political leaders. This phase is till September 2014. His horoscope is similar to Tilak and Bismarck.

All the Hindi language Dailies have portrayed the image of Modi in their own way and analysed his profile. Some journalists remarked in their own inimitable style. Vinit Narayan of Punjab Kesari wrote, "In the past ten years, a large section of media has been attacking Modi trying to gain their selfish motives like getting a Padmshree, membership of Rajya Sabha or financial assistance for their TV channel. There was also a sting operation in 2007 but all these attempts were futile. The present breed of journalists were basking in their own glory and living in a fool's paradise that the common man is ignorant and they would not understand their games but the common man emphatically asserted himself and told them that their opinions are not influenced by media but he forms it based on his ability to understand and analyse the real issues." Vinit Narayan adds, "During the last 10 years whenever a large section of the media attacked Modi on some issue, I raised some questions against these journalists belonging to 22 various states. I wanted to tell them that with every attack, Modi was gaining popularity. This is because he was doing things which the people expect from a leader. The results are before everyone to see. It is another matter that people who change their colour like a chameleon will not hesitate now to sing his praises. Modi also consistently ignored such people and proved that he was passionate about achieving his goals and he would not stop until they materialise.

Tarun Vijay writes, "History has been created' is an understatement. It feels as though the soldiers of 1857 revolt for freedom have won after 157 years and we are free from the evil shadow of the British. This is not only change of power but this is a transformation in Political philosophy, passions and expression. The anger against politics of corruption and ego which was deeply in the hearts of common people has found an expression by instilling faith in Modi. This is the threshold of peoples' revolt which has restored the structure of democracy, saved its grace and in the end the burden and feudalism of Nehru –Gandhi family legacy has been overthrown. The bureaucracy and Government during the UPA regime had taken people for granted and considered the assets of the nation as their personal wealth. They had adopted the policy of managing the media, bribe them, help them by giving advertisements and they thought that they could appease the voters in this manner. The ego of Congress reflected in their insult of Manmohan Singh. The 'prince' insulted him repeatedly. They maintained an eerie silence on serious issues like corruption. They created two power centres. They overlooked the misdeeds of its cadre. They made personal attacks on the opposition. They indulged in the politics of abuses and character assassination. What was the end result? The voters decided that if they did not teach them a lesson, even God would not be able to protect them."

Tarun Modi, while parsing the personality of Modi added that he would become a famous international leader like Putin of Russia, Obama of USA and Xi Jin Ping of China. Not only would the national image improve but the safety, security and self-respect of our armed forces, borders and common man would see better days. However, our first priority would be improvement in the economic condition and firming up the exchange rate of rupee. We face the stiff challenge of achieving overall growth rate of 8% of our GDP. The manufacturing sector of the country passing through a very critical phase. We are forced to import small and big equipments from China. Therefore, we have the enormous responsibility to strengthen this sector. It is necessary that the common man has an easy access to education establishing benchmarks of excellence also needs to be given priority. Equally large is the challenge of offering a good price to the farmer for his produce. We must ensure that equipment for irrigation to reach at every corner. Be it drinking water or rural electrification, roads or railway tracks, in a way, Modi will have to work very hard for the revival of spirit of the nation. Every attack and lie was used to alienate and slander Modi but in the end the feelings of public won. Modi emerged as leader. This has astounded everyone in the world. His emergence will make India to emerge as powerful and proud nation on this earth."

He writes further, "It is noteworthy that two people who were groomed in the stables of RSS and who imbibed its values emerged as the Prime Minister of India. One of them was Atal Bihari Vajpayee who established new records in the political history of India and the other one is Modi who was a pracharak, a propagator, a volunteer who will also establish new benchmarks. He is also a strong proponent of this saffron passion. He too has huge ambitions which he has been nurturing with restraint. More than the external challenges, the inner rivalries, the huge spate of unfulfilled expectations, and dreams are bound to make the journey after 16th May more arduous but for someone who has faced the deplorable attacks at global level, who has persistently passed the acid test of conquering the opposition and who has been successful in getting the blessings of the abode of Kashi Vishveshwar, success is imminent. It is a foregone conclusion that the movement of breaking the ego of the elite and of high and mighty has reached a final stage. Where everyone who was considered untouchable in every possible intellectual and physical manner, is now moving towards unfurling the tricolour flag on the red fort. This is a new party of activists who break the casteist intellectual embargo. You must accept them."

Balendu Sharma Dadhich wrote on Prabhasakshi.com, "A new era has dawned in the National Democratic Alliance and BJP by the virtue of their unprecedented win. For the first time in the last six decades, a non-Congress party has come to power with a clear majority. In fact, it has established its roots in the entire nation. BJP was considered as a party which dominated the main stream Hindi belt. This was considered to be a major roadblock in its becoming a mainstream party to come to power. It was thought that it did not enjoy the support in the East and South. The party led by Modi has proven all these equations wrong. It has established itself as a national level party in the true sense. It became stronger in the states where it was already in power. The entire Hindi belt now adorns a saffron colour all over but even in the states where the presence of BJP was minimal, with these results, it has proved its mettle. As it stands today, only three states, Tamil Nadu, West Bengal and Orissa still have the hold of its regional parties. However, in the coming years, BJP is bound to establish itself in these states also.

The media analysed this win in many ways. There was a plethora of all kinds of explanations and analyses before and after elections but in the end, it was Modi and Modi alone.

Important interviews

'I dream of not becoming something but of doing something'

Narendra Modi's first candid and matchless interview with the editor of 'Naya India', Hari Shankar Vyas, was his first interview with the media after he became the PM where he elaborated at great length about his vision and thoughts on changing the fortunes of India. What is the vision and what is the action plan to fulfil it? And what is the guarantee that he puts into practice what he plans and thinks about? He also spoke about his thoughts about various sections of the society. He also talked about a few aspects of his personal life, lifestyle and way of working. He also told about his philosophy of life. We reproduce the interview.

Question- At the outset, I urge you to speak from your heart and speak frankly, without inhibitions. The very purpose of this talk is to understand your vision, your thoughts about the country, what you plan to do, how do you plan to achieve your vision? How will you write the destiny of the nation? So, my first question is, why have you given the slogan of 'Congress-free India?' Why not, corruption-free India, unemployment-free India or poverty-free India? Wouldn't it be better?

NM-You have asked me to be frank and honest. I have one satisfaction; the country knows me at least for one thing: whenever Modi speaks, he speaks frankly, without inhibitions, from heart and with conviction. I really feel happy and relaxed when it comes to speaking the truth.

When I speak about 'Congress-free India', I mean freedom from the work-culture that the Congress has given to this nation during the last sixty years. The culture it has nurtured. By this, I mean freedom from the politics of vote bank, the politics of grabbing power through any means. The country hasn't witnessed such a vulgar display of corruption which it has during the last ten years. Thus, a Congress-free India necessarily means an India free from bad governance, free from the dynastic rule, free from the misuse of constitutional institutions, free from inflation, free from crises of different kinds. The Congress has become a synonym for all these problems. But, I want a 'Congress-free India' by democratic means.

Question- But during the last sixty years, there has been three such occasions when India became 'Congress-free'. There were non-Congress governments at the centre. But broadly, it was just the change of faces. The governments were run in the typical Congress style. How will it be different this time?

You are absolutely correct. Except Atal ji's government, others were headed by people from the Congress Gotra- their clan. They were born in the Congress culture. They grew up in the Congress culture but left the party due to their personal ambitions.You can see a clear distinction in the government run by Atalji. He brought an entirely different culture and had a clear and nationalist vision. His politics was based on different ideals. He was a man with different ideology, culture and values.

Question- Yet, it also failed to change the fundamentals of governance, may be due to the system that prevailed in Delhi. What is your vision to deal with such roadblocks?

When I took over in Gujarat, it was the same situation there too. Exactly the same system, the same employees, same files and same traditions. Yet there have been changes; distinctive changes. Good governance depends on the will of the policy makers. It depends on their commitment; the way schemes are formulated and executed. Therefore, it is not the system that is critical; it is the person who runs it. Can you change the work force over-night? Two crores of people! No. You have to run the system. You must have seen even in your channel that whenever there is a change at the top, the entire format of programming changes. Owner remains the same and so do the employees. But the entire look, output and presentation of the channel changes.

Question- But when the system remains the same, runs on those same old lines, even the leadership fails. Even good editors cannot change the face of the channel! Don't you think that it is imperative to bring in some fundamental changes in the system?

It seems that you are a pessimist and therefore such type of thoughts will bother your mind. But I am an optimist. I work with confidence. And have learnt all these things from my experience. I do believe that the people of this great nation are not bad. The system is not bad. If they get the right kind of leadership, they will follow the right path.

Question- So, in the light of shortcomings of the UPA regime, its wrong-doings, its mishandling of the situation, what is your perception regarding the current crisis and what is your vision, your blueprint?

What is the biggest crisis facing the nation? First and foremost, People have lost their confidence not only in the Congress or the institution of the Prime Minister, but in the very institution of the government which is so crucial to run the country. No nation can survive without a sense of confidence. So the foremost priority is to restore their confidence in the system, to bring them out from an environment of trust-deficit. And this election of 2014 does not leave any scope for negativity. This is an 'election for hope'. This is happening for the first time in India.

Question- But there has been a sense of mistrust in the nation about the political leadership and the political system in the past four years. How will you restore this trust and confidence among the people?

People of the country know Modi very well. Vajpayee-led NDA government's intentions and performance is still fresh in their minds. The manner in which the BJP-led governments operate in their states is also too well known. They can distinguish between the NDA and Congress rules. Sterling performance of the BJP governments in Chhattisgarh, Madhya Pradesh and Goa have rekindled their hopes. It's the cumulative effect that people in every nook and corner of the country believe that the BJP's intentions are good and honest and they want to work for the poor. Today, the governments of Rajasthan, Gujarat, Madhya Pradesh and Chhattisgarh have got an opportunity to serve 40% of the total tribal population in the country. The governments headed by Vasundhara ji, Shivraj ji, Raman Singh ji have instilled a sense of confidence and trust by their schemes and actions in the society that the BJP doesn't believe in making hollow promises. It gives results. It works for the poor.

Question- So, you believe that it is the cumulative effect of all the BJP led governments (including yours), and of course, your leadership qualities. Given all these, the people of the country have great expectations from you and your party. Have you drawn a roadmap to achieve the target in a given time-frame?

Absolutely! Yes. My priorities are clear in my mind as to what my policies and programmes will be for the poor. What will I do to pull out from the existing system? How to infuse life into it? How to make it dynamic? How to instill a sense of self-esteem in the people of the country? It's all very clear in my mind.

Question- But the moot question is how can a government at the national level have a focus on such small things, issues? How is it possible?

As I said earlier, the policies should be clear, unambiguous. When I say that people must get clean and pure drinking water, it may appear to be a small issue, but it needs a big thinking at the national level. But some people think that only if you speak of an airplane only then you would be thinking big, and not by thinking about a cycle for everyone in the village.

Question- But is it possible to implement such small things at the national level?

With 12 years of experience, I can assert that I am known for implementation. That is what I believe in and stand for.

Question- What do you attribute the place that you occupy today and you aspire to occupy tomorrow – your fate or your purusharth- your capability? Did you ever dream of it?

The people of this country will decide my destiny. I have never dreamt to become something. But have always dreamt of doing something. To achieve those dreams, I have decided to dedicate myself to the service of the nation. I left my family and my village to achieve this goal. My country is my motherland and its 1.25 billion population is my family. The entire nation knows where I was born, how I was brought up and I have strong faith in this present life. I always want to tell the youth of this country that they should not dream of becoming something. I too never dreamt of becoming something in my life. Even today as I talk to you, I want to repeat that I did not dream of becoming something in my life. You should dream of doing something. You should sacrifice your entire life to fulfill this dream. What should I be doing? I should serve my country, its downtrodden, have-nots, troubled and tribals. I left my home to serve them. This is my mission. India is my motherland and its countrymen are my family. I have been brought up by this family and it is my dream to do something for them. Even today, on 27th, I am not dreaming to become someone but to achieve something. To become someone is a very small achievement but to achieve something is a big act. I am not a hero. He runs the Government only to win elections. We want to form and run a Government to give strength to the society. They aim at grabbing power while we concentrate on empowerment and that is our final goal.

Question- There is a general feeling that you have turned this election into a presidential kind of election. And, therefore, people see in you an image of a NAYAK- a hero. It's natural that they would also be interested in knowing what will be your vision for different fields, what will be your priorities?

First thing, I do not consider myself a NAYAK, a hero; nor do I think in this direction. I have a commitment towards the nation, towards it people. Who are my priorities? They are the poorest of the poor; the youth of the nation who is in despair today; the women of this country who are feeling insecure; our farmers, our forces on the borders. Late Lal Bahadur Shastri had given us a slogan, 'Jai Jawan, Jai Kisan'. But the way they are decapitated and the farmers are forced to commit suicide; it seems that the Congress has changed it to 'Mar Jawan, Mar Kisan' .

They (the Congress) have brought the nation to this sorry state of affairs. In such circumstances, our priorities must change. Employment to the youth and their skill development is a priority in the entire world. Do we need to set up an extraordinary commission in the country for enabling skill development? It just needs a commitment. All we need is facilitating skill development for our youth. Give them opportunities for employment. If you live in Delhi and need a plumber, you won't get one. On the other hand, there are crores of youth in search of job. Why not train them to meet your requirements? These are small things but make a big difference. The successive governments have not paid any heed to these small issues. They have only indulged in the politics of vote bank. The result is for all to see.

Question- You means if the present schemes are implemented honestly, many of the problems will be solved?

Yes, but their approach, schemes are all directed at the politics of vote bank. They run the government only with an eye on the elections. On the other hand, we want to run the government to empower the people of this country.

Question- How do you perceive all these thinking, policies and programmes in the framework of your blueprint, ideology?

I will give you an example. Is it not the need of the hour that the productivity of our land must increase? Our size of holding is small and it is not likely to grow either. If we want to make our farmer self-reliant, we will have to multiply the productivity manifold. Our yield per acre must increase. We just need to create a system to take care of the health of his soil. Make a health-card for his farm. Educate him about the health of his soil. In the absence of such a system, he would use fertilizers randomly and pesticides indiscriminately. He does not know as for which crop his piece of land is suitable. He needs a scientific back up. He does not know which fertilizer is good for his farm. He is ignorant and adds pesticides with incomplete knowledge.

Same is the fate of infrastructure for irrigation. It is the misfortune of the country that it still lacks in irrigation infrastructure even after over six decades of independence. Atalji had taken a lead in this direction. He envisioned linking of rivers across the country. If there are floods or droughts we will be saved. The losses which we incur each year can be prevented. But the UPA government put it in the cold storage. Now the Supreme Court has taken them to task for sitting duck over this scheme. We can interlink rivers – big and small and create a network. If the rivers were interlinked, we would be spared of the misery of floods as well as drought. These long term plans must be given priority so that all the lost time can be made up very quickly. Speed is the essence and must be prioritized. I will put in special efforts.

Question- That means you have made a specific vision for the agriculture and irrigation sectors?

Yes, absolutely. Gujarat was never counted among the agricultural states. But today, we have carved a place for ourselves in this sector. The same way, we made strides in the milk sector. Unfortunately, this revolution remained confined to Gujarat. There is need for synergy between agriculture and animal husbandry to raise the income of the farmers. We must explore how all this can be made viable. How do we make our husbandry viable? How do we increase the income?

Secondly, agriculture sector cannot be seen in isolation. It has to be done in a holistic manner. There are three activities in this sector that can be merged together to make it a viable and profitable pursuit – the first is farming, second is animal husbandry and the third, growing trees on the fences. Today we are importing timber. This will be stopped. The last will reduce our dependence on imports of timber over a period of time.

We need to think new. It is the misfortune of the country that the poor farmer has to resort to distress-sale of his produce in the absence of storage facilities. Even expression of annoyance and displeasure by the Supreme Court fails to move this insensitive government. They let the crop rot and finally the poor farmer has to sell it to distilleries for a pittance. We know how large a pain it causes to the farmer. Nobody can even guess how much damage it causes to the youth of the nation. Therefore we must think of changing the system. Progress should be such that it provides opportunity to everyone.

Question-The present generation is craving for value for merit. Reservation should take a back seat. What's your view on this?

Look, when I came to Gujarat, there were 13 thousand seats in engineering. There were tensions on the issue of reservation. Today, there are over one lakh seats. The problem of reservation has vanished. The development should be such that everybody gets an opportunity. Nobody is interested in grabbing. But if we don't provide opportunities, what will they do? Every poor, a Dalit or a tribal or anybody for that matter, must get his right.

Question-Today we have a plethora of irrelevant laws which need to be reformed. What is your opinion about law and order and Police administration?

At times I tend to believe that lawlessness is a fact but it is also necessary to have fewer laws. On one hand you have lawlessness and on the other we should have fewer laws. I feel that we are lost in the labyrinth of laws. We are still following archaic laws which came into existence in 19th and 18th century. The world has changed drastically. The more we simplify them, more we will be set free. Secondly, there is a difference between rules and administration. It has many aspects. One of them is Human Resource Development of the Police force. We must modernize it. Today a six feet tall young man joins the Police force; he then does some march-past and drill for nine months and at the end of it he is given a gun and he is also told about the laws. We have done an experiment in Gujarat. For the first time we have established a 'Raksha Shakti University'. Those who want to join security forces, want to wear a uniform will graduate from there and if he scores good marks, then he would be taught about laws, law and order , they will be trained about handling of arms. He will be trained about Legal Psychology, women's rights and thus a very capable cadre will pass out. When such people join the Police force, there would be a gradual transformation. This can be done on a large scale.

Secondly, the nature of crime has changed today. Crime has become complex by use of Technology. Cyber-crime is on the increase. Economic crimes too have seen a rise. If one has to investigate such crimes, the investigator too must know the Technology. We will have to emphasize on Forensic medicine. Gujarat is the first state where the first Forensic Science University has been established. Many colleges elsewhere have a Forensic Science department but this is the first Forensic University in the world. We also train judges there. We teach lawyers and police about the protocol under which the cases of rape are to be investigated. The victim will be examined with full dignity. Only when we adopt such modern practices, we will be able to bring transformation. Merely making laws for the sake of getting votes will not lead us anywhere.

Question- What is your vision of national issues, particularly security and foreign policy?

The central government has failed on every front. Be it the internal front or the external front. On the issues of foreign policy, defence or internal security, have we ever seen tension anywhere in the world between the Defence Minister and the armed forces? Even in Indira Gandhi's regime, was there ever any differentiation in the forces on the basis of religion; Hindu or Muslim?

Our submarines are drowning. Our jawans are being killed. The decision making process has come to a standstill. We have failed to modernize our defence equipments. There is an urgent need to modernize our forces and to inculcate discipline among them. Strained relationship between the government and the armed forced is unacceptable.

With hostile China and Pakistan on our borders, have we realized what will happen after US forces leave Afghanistan? Have we anticipated impending troubles on our borders? Are we ready to face these challenges? The problem is that the UPA does not have a vision. It does not have a commitment to the nation. National security is not their priority. I hold the entire government and the NSC responsible for this sorry state of affairs. We spend billions of dollars every year to import defence equipment. Cannot we help the youth of this country manufacture such equipment in India? Why can't we adopt a progressive and aggressive policy on this front? Can't we urge and facilitate our industry and engineering colleges to work for manufacturing these equipments indigenously? We should manufacture equipments to meet our requirements. We should become an exporting nation instead of depending on imports.

Question- Under such circumstances, do you believe that a good leader can set right the functioning of various departments?

Yes, he can. He has to set guidelines and should create a mechanism to monitor it. He should instil a sense of commitment and confidence among the staff and officers of the departments by personal contact, communication and confidence building measures. Their morale needs to be boosted. Their suggestions should be appreciated.

It is one thing to sit in an ivory tower and take a 'hands free' approach but it alienates the leader from the real issues.

This is what has been the main problem with UPA. They are far away from the people who work for the nation. They do not get an opportunity to express themselves.

Neither their good work known to the decision makers nor are they held accountable. This widens the rift between.

I will make efforts to streamline this by setting a personal example.

I will put in hard work till the things are streamlined and thus set an example. I also wish to be accessible, far away from the bureaucracy and red-tapism

Shorten the winding process of seeking justice through archaic laws!

Economic reforms are those which bring a whiff of fresh air and rejuvenate. They start a new thought process. It creates opportunities for people. Our files travel circuitous route and yet they do not see a conclusive decision being taken. This must stop.

Why don't we synchronise all the systems and processes? Secondly, technology must be used to usher an era of transparency.

Question- What are your views on economic reforms and how do we get over the obstacles in its way? How do we accelerate the pace of reforms?

The programmes which are cunningly designed to attract the vote bank but which, in reality, are a drain on the treasury are being flouted as an economic reforms but they are not as they are called. Economic reforms are those which bring life into the entire system. They mark the beginning of a new thought process. We are getting entangled in the jungle of laws. The need of the hour is that this jungle is de-weeded and the rules should be simplified. Process should be made shorter. In our Hindu philosophy, we say that if you visit the four pilgrimage centres, you will attain salvation. But in our offices, files go on perennial pilgrimage and yet they do not attain salvation. This has to stop. Technology must bring transparency. All the systems and processes must be synchronized. Files remain pending for signatures. Why do we have to change the Minister? It is such a serious matter and if we make extensive use of technology, be it e- procurement or e –tendering, reduce human intervention, faster and easier it would be. Countries from all over the world will start trusting us.

Question- Does all this fall under the parameters of good governance?

It is not only a matter of good governance but it is a part of long term actions and form a part of thought process for progress.

Question- To support all this macro and micro level economic philosophy and to implement it do you have something like a think tank?

All my countrymen are my think-tank. My centuries old legacy is my think tank. The changing world, new technologies, research and innovation are my commitments and everyone associated with these is my guide. The suggestion of even a man on the street is important to me, his words mean a lot to me and at times even a poor farmer in a village can provide tremendous impetus and strength to transform the nation.

Question- Does it mean that you will work in Delhi only as guided by your valuable philosophy and experience and not to trust the suggestions of Planning Commission?

Please do not put your words and thoughts in my mouth and erode my mind. These are your suggestions.

Question- People have so many expectations from you that on the social media one can see that when you become the Prime Minister, the dollar would be equivalent to Rs 40 and petrol will sell at Rs. 50. Do you ever feel the burden of such expectations? Can these be fulfilled?

After all, why have such expectations risen? Are these not reasonable? Shouldn't be Indian rupee strong in the world market? Shouldn't we find the ways to combat inflation? Their expectations are not to bring in stars from the sky. They are not asking for Rolls Royce in front of their houses. They are asking for basic minimum things. It is the responsibility of the government to provide its people basic amenities after sixty years of independence. Seven years from now, we shall be celebrating the Platinum Jubilee of the Independence. A time has come to introspect whether we can give our martyrs the India of their dreams for which they sacrificed their lives? We ought to resolve now that we will give Indians a nation of the dreams of our great leaders. This way, we can also connect with the crores of people of the country.

The agenda for development is not the government's agenda. It is the agenda of the countrymen. Shastriji had connected himself with the countrymen when he gave the nation the slogan 'Jai Jawan, Jai Kisan'. At that time, we used to import wheat from abroad. He urged farmers in the country to grow more to meet the domestic demands. His appeal that came from his heart had a magical effect and the same farmers made India self-sufficient in no time. Wheat is not grown in the government offices. It was the sincerity of the leadership and people's confidence in it that produced wonders. This is how changes can be brought about. One needs to understand the strength of the 1.25 billion strong countrymen. We are fortunate that 65% of our population is younger than 35 years of age. Entire world envies us. The leadership should provide opportunities to fulfil the dreams of the youth.

Question- Today, you have emerged as a leader who connects with the dreams of the youth. They have high expectations from you. But you will appreciate that the youth loses their patience very fast. If they don't get results soon, there could be serious consequences.

No. I do not subscribe to this view. Today's generation understands and analyses the situation dispassionately. I cannot analyze like them. The generation has changed. If they are convinced about the intentions and convictions of the leadership, they would never lose their patience. Please do not underestimate their ability to understand the situations and of reasoning. Just have faith. You just need to remain connected. We must trust them. It is necessary to have a connect. If we can achieve this, they can lead the nation. The strength of our youth is their analytical power.

Question- Apart from this, what will be your priority for him – education or employment?

The foremost thing is employment. Jobless growth is the biggest crisis staring in our face. UPA is notorious for this. What should be the parameters of development? Creation of jobs should commensurate with the growth in the agricultural sector or the industrial sector. If we want growth in this sector then commensurate with growth in crops, employment too must increase.

Tourism industry has such a large potential for employment generation. Tourism is going to directly benefit the youth. Today, the irony is that we have to outsource our developmental activities. We lay very little emphasis on research. Research and innovation should be our priorities. We lag behind in the matter of patent registration. We do not focus on research and innovation. Many paradigms in the world have changed. Do not we have enough talent? If we provide congenial atmosphere for our youth, they can excel in the fields of IPR and holding patents.

I have been brought up in RSS with the values of living and dying for the nation and to follow discipline at all costs. I have been given the doctrine of hard work and service of the downtrodden. I believe that hard work with innovation can make tremendous impact. This, complemented by honesty, holds the key to the progress of the nation.

I trust that these qualities have to become the backbone of our country. I have been lucky to be groomed like this and I am grateful to RSS for imbibing these in me.

Question- People know you for your determination. You left your family to become a pracharak- a volunteer propagator. What transformation do you see in yourself over these years?

First of all the child's foundation for life is laid when he studies in lower classes. This foundation makes him a very big scientist or a Nobel Prize winner, an engineer, a doctor or a soldier.

I have been brought up in the RSS tradition with the values of living and dying for the nation and to follow discipline at all costs. I believe that hard work with innovation can make tremendous impact. Even today, when I travel and at the end of the day when people ask me if I am tired, I just smile because I have been brought up in this way.

This, complemented by honesty holds the key to the progress of the nation.

Question- It all started with a penchant for social work. How did it convert to politics?

Even today, politics is not an ambition for me. It's a mission. It's not rajniti- a mere Strategy that is important to me; it is rashtraniti- Strategy for nation. Power is not everything for us. Service of the society is everything. These are the samskaras- values imbibed in us. Whatever we do, I will do with sense of responsibility. India should regain the status of Jagatguru (teacher of the world). This should be our dream. That should be the dream of every Indian.

Question- When you left home, freed yourself from all worldly ties and joined RSS, did you have this in your mind?

From that very day, I had decided that if I get an opportunity to serve even one poor soul, I shall do it. If get an opportunity to serve 50, I would serve 50 and if I have to serve half a million, I will do it. Numbers really did not matter. Scale may change but not my determination. What matters in life is clarity of goal and zeal to accomplish it, the readiness to struggle and stand undeterred.

Question- In all these opportunities, how much would you attribute to luck or destiny and how much to hard work?

I believe that this nation has dire need of these – Neta, Neeti and Neeyat. If all these are in place then fortune too would be on your side.

Question- I have seen your political journey of 25 to 30 years. I believe that you have been very fortunate. Is there any divine power which entitles you to be the candidate for PM in spite of adverse circumstances? If your appointment as the CM of Gujarat was no strange coincidence and ever since you became the CM, then there has not been any natural calamity. You saw good rainfall every year. You found opportunities in every act of opposition from your rivals. Is this some kind of a divine or providential blessing? Do you trust in God? Do you pray every day?

I believe in God. I have faith. I believe in supreme power but I also believe that I should not bother Him. I should try to accomplish everything for which He has sent me here. I should not expect Him to do it. Don't keep pestering Him asking for favours. Do pray every day. We must follow the path of virtuousness. God will bestow wisdom of distinguishing right from wrong and we must lead our path based on this wisdom.

Question- Who has been your role model since your childhood?

I have been influenced by the philosophy of Swami Vivekananda since my childhood. We had a library in my village where I used to read. I would borrow books there. These books were on patriotism. Vivekananda was a sage and a believer. He believed in the Supreme-being. But he said often that we should forget about Him and remember only Mother India. This appealed to me. He used to say service to the poor is service to God. When you help the poor, you are doing His work. Vivekananda said play football; think about Geeta only after this. These were revolutionary thoughts and I liked them.

Question- What is your vision about the industrial and employment sectors?

We have vast opportunities for industrial and employment sectors. But we need to prioritize them first. Why don't we give a boost to the agro-industry sector? It's high time that we lay our emphasis on value addition of agricultural produce. Our farmer does not get the value for his money when he sells raw tomatoes. But if he sells it to the ketchup industry, his income will go up and it will also generate employment.

Then, we have a vast expanse of the sea coast. A burgeoning industry in the world is the ship-building industry which requires sea coast. If it can flourish in a country like Korea, why not in India? It does not need a very skilled labour; just some turners, fitters, welders, etc.

Question- Since you have spoken of right, what is your focus on the right to health and medical facilities?

First thing is that we are still stuck at health insurance while the need is of health assurance. Second, while we are worried about our illness, we do not pay heed to keep good health. Preventive healthcare should be our priority. If people get clean and pure drinking water, the incidence of diseases will come down. If school children are taught small but basic things like hygiene, they will not fall ill. All through his life, Gandhiji paid so much attention on the issue of hygiene. In five years from now when we celebrate his 150th anniversary, we should pay him a tribute in the form of a clean India. If we do not make any compromise with hygiene, health sector will get a big boost.

The other problem is that of paucity of doctors. Today, we do not have even 10 percent of doctors as compared to our requirements. We do not have sufficient number of medical colleges. Why can't we have a medical college in each district? A college built on PPP model can also bring in a hospital in each district. If the youth gets an opportunity to stay in the vicinity of his village, there will be no dearth of doctors in the rural areas. Human resource is as important as infrastructure. The third thing is availability of medicines at reasonable prices. If we lay adequate emphasis on indigenous research, we can provide medicines at cheaper rates. Then, optimal use of infrastructure is another big issue. In the government hospitals, operation theaters work only in single shift. More shifts at the same infrastructure can bring major change. Thus a sum of small-small things can bring in major changes.

Question- You have been laying great emphasis on women's empowerment. What do you have to say about reservation for them?

We gave 50% reservation to women in our panchayats. But the bill is pending with the Governor for months and years. Irony is that the Governor herself is a woman. She is sitting over it while we are committed for it.

But more important is to work for eliminating gender discrimination. This will have to be done at the social level, on cultural level, by changing the education system. This discrimination will have to be erased from our mindset.

Question- Which is your favourite book, which helped formulate your views, which influenced you?

In my early childhood, when I was in the village, I was an avid reader. But a stage came, when I could not read further. Unfortunately, I don't get time for reading.

Question- What are your other interests? Films, music...?

Yes, lot of interests. I like listening to music.

Question- Classical or popular?

It depends. I like instrumental music more. It touches my soul. I believe that while the western music makes you dance, the Indian music stirs your soul. And you like what stirs your soul. I also like roaming in the hills and mountains. The Himalayas have been my most favourite destination. But these are no longer my priorities.

Question- Your lifestyle, your dress, your interests, your home, your office look little different from others. Where did you inherit such tastes?

A lot of myths have been created around me. No one has ever bothered to look deeper into them. I will give you an example. It dates back to those years when NDA was in power and I was a general secretary of the party. The editor of a big newspaper called me at 7.30 in the morning and said that he wanted to meet me. I asked him to come to Ashok Road around 11. But when he said that he was standing outside my office, I called him in.

When he entered my room, I was wearing a saffron lungi. And used to sleep on my blanket. Some newspapers were lying scattered around the blanket. There were some books. A copper decanter had some water in it. And there was a plastic chair lying in the room. I asked him if he would like to have some tea. He said, yes. I got up and went outside to the footpath to fetch a cup of tea.

After he had tea, I asked him as to what brought him here so early in the day? He looked worried. Normally, journalists do not wake up so early. At first, he was reluctant to open up. But when I insisted, he said that his magazine was doing a story on those RSS pracharaks (propagators) who had moved to the BJP. The idea was that their lifestyles had changed ever since they came to politics. I asked him what he thought after seeing me. He said that they were wrong. Then, I asked him whether they would do the story now? But it's the misfortune of the country that the story got killed. I wear these simple glasses, but people would say that it is of a big brand, very expensive! I wear simple Khadi. But I like an orderly living. And if something suits my physique, it gets a brand name!

Question- You mean, your lifestyle is natural and there is nothing artificial in it?

I am so surprised and sad that if one lives neat and clean and in an orderly manner, many things are attributed to him.

Question- What has been the happiest moment of your life, and the saddest?

The happiest moment is yet to arrive. When the poorest or poor has a house to live, elders will have access to medicines, education for all, farmers will not be forced to commit suicide, there will be no unemployment- that will be the happiest moment of my life. No rest till then.

Question- And the saddest moment?

I do not count my sad moments. I do not waste time on that

Question- You boast of the legacy of the RSS. There, they work in a team, take collective decisions. But in your case, there is a general perception that you believe in going alone, taking your decisions without consulting your colleagues...?

This is another big lie about me. Since they are unable to trap me with any serious charges, they spread such rumours about me. Can a single person bring such a big change in a large state like Gujarat? It could not have been achieved without the effort of the Team Gujarat. If you don't have a good team, if you don't listen to it, you cannot succeed. The secret of my success is that I listen to my team, work in tandem with its members. And once we reach a consensus, I work with full force to implement it.

Question- Did you work with this spirit during the last eight months also?

I have been learning this since my adolescent days. I don't know any other way of working. My success is attributed to listening to everyone, to work with everyone. But people who do not like Modi, they play such things.

Harishankar Vyas- Modi Ji, Many-Many Thanks!

Modi- You are welcome.

Modi's interview to Navbharat Times

The election campaign which lasted little over two months, heard incessant chant of 'Namo, Namo'. It was obvious that whereas NDA was presenting the Prime Ministerial candidate as a hero, the UPA rivals did not leave any stone unturned in proving him to be a villain. In the entire history of Indian Democracy, accusations and allegations were not made at the rival party in general but its Prime Ministerial candidate was targeted in particular thus making it a central figure of criticism. This only helped in Modi assuming a larger than life image. A lot of bitterness and personal rivalry could be seen in the campaign. What does Modi think of it? If he became the PM, what would be his roadmap? In an exclusive interview, Navbharat Times editors Gulshanrai Khatri and Narendranath asked many questions of vital importance to Modi. We reproduce some excerpts.

NBT: Bitterness between various political parties has increased during the election campaign. Could it have been avoided? Can the effect of this be seen in the coming days affecting the relationship between the Govt and opposition parties?

NM: It is true that as the tempo of election canvassing picked up, our opposition parties have crossed all the limits in their speeches and statements. Especially, overawed by the massive turnout and heavy polling in the initial stages, Congress and its allies did not hesitate to hurl abuses. Right from the beginning we had decided that we would fight the elections on positive issues like progress and good governance. If the other political parties also had cooperated with us, it would have been a new beginning in the annals of election politics. Unfortunately, our opponents spent all their energy in tilting the campaign towards old issues like casteism and communalism. In addition, this is the first election which is being fought by a big party like BJP on all important issues like progress and good governance. During the last six months I have make sincere and serious attempts to implement this. The prediction of media that the effect of those will be seen after the election is an exaggerated thought. In fact it is not so at the ground level. It is often seen that the leaders who ruthlessly attack each other during the campaign, greet and talk to each other with comfort and ease when they accidently meet each other on some airport. It is not that the fights and differences of opinion affect the personal relations adversely. After they warmly meet each other, when they go back to the rallies, the usual practice of allegations and counter allegations also continues. One must understand that there is competition in Politics but it never culminates into enmity. I also feel sorry for one more development. Light hearted harmless fun and humour is slowly diminishing from public life. It is also very necessary to have some humour and fun along with seriousness in public life and there should be no place for indifference to personal relationship. One must realize that we politicians occupy a large space in cartoons, jokes and become a target of ridicule too. These days we see a lot of moral policing too. This is required but only within limits. Its excessive use is unwarranted. As far as the coming days are concerned, we will neither work with a sense of revenge nor take the electoral rivalry beyond the days of campaign. We will carry out all our duties with humility and we will also be seeking the cooperation of our colleagues in opposition to take the nation on a path of progress.

NBT: If you are elected to power, what expectations should the country have from you? Will you take opposition along with you and if so what steps would you take to get their cooperation?

NM-We ensure that we will work hard to fulfill peoples' expectations from us. It will be our relentless endeavor to work hard, day and night, to provide good administration and take the nation on the path of progress. It is necessary to have an alert opposition to ensure nation's progress and for strengthening the democracy. One can understand the possibility of opposition based on issues and therefore we will always be ready to discuss with an open mind. To ensure consensus will be a part of our style of working.

NBT: This nation adopted liberal economic policies from the nineties. Will these continue? Or is there a need to change them as a need of the hour?

NM: Any nation or society cannot make progress if it remains static. Every nation needs to make timely changes to ensure survival and growth. To ensure rapid and continuous pace of progress, the economic system also needs to improve. We will take all the necessary steps which will accelerate pace of development, improve its condition and generate employment.

NBT: What is your opinion about GST and FDI in multi-brand retail? Should this happen or not?

NM: GST is a simple and an excellent solution to increase revenues. GST has been stalled because of the partial treatment states get in terms of the aid they get. However, our Govt will remove all the obstacles in the way of implementation of GST and play a positive role in removing corruption and possibilities of unreasonable delays. It is necessary to establish a nationwide infrastructure of IT network for effective implementation of GST but UPA Govt did not make any efforts in this direction. In all critical matters, there have been delays or I can say that UPA created a situation of policy paralysis and developed a sick mentality of defaming the State Governments for any failure. As far as FDI in multi-brand retail is concerned, we have very clearly mentioned our official stand in our election manifesto.

NBT: You have often advocated starting of bullet trains and setting up new cities. These will no doubt accelerate the pace of nation's progress but where will you get funds for such large investmemts? It is estimated that just to run one bullet train on Mumbai-Ahmedabad track, it will require Rs 60,000 crores. Do you think running of such expensive trains all over the country be economically viable and successful?

NM: It is the misfortune of our nation that the Governments which ruled this country considered poverty as a boon rather than a bane. They felt it was a glorious necessity. May be it was the need of vote bank politics or maybe there was lack of long term vision. The ultimate result is that we can neither think big nor make any efforts to become world-class. On the other hand, countries like South Korea which were in a similar plight like ours at the time of our independence have scaled peaks of progress only due to their expansive thinking. Atal ji's government had started an important mission like launching of Golden Quadrilateral. It was a magnificent beginning in the direction of providing world class infrastructure to Indian population. Unfortunately in the last ten years, instead of making progress, it has been pushed back in oblivion. I strongly believe that if your vision is big and if you are prepared to work hard with full capability then our nation too can move ahead on the path of progress. We can also gradually provide world class infrastructure to our citizens. As far as funding is considered, I do not think that in the present times, it would be difficult to get money.

NBT: Are you aware of India's relationship with its neighbouring countries including Pakistan Do you have any plans in your mind to improve these ties? If yes, what are they?

NM: Today, when terrorism has rocked the entire world and when our country is fighting on many fronts, it is necessary in such circumstances that we plan a strategy to establish a base of healthy and strong ties to combat terrorism. As long as any neighbour promotes terrorism against India, it is difficult to maintain good relations. I believe that our foreign policy should be based on mutual trust and friendship. Similarly our relations with other nations should also be based upon equality and mutual understanding. National interest should be uppermost in our minds. Neither do we want to threaten anyone nor do we want that anyone should threaten us. We wish that we should be able to look into each other's eyes and should talk straightway.

NBT: You keep talking about establishing team spirit between PM and CM at centre and state level but how can this happen when you have opposition ruled Govts at state level? If yes, how will you give a new face to centre-state relationship and how will it look?

NM: I feel that Team India must include PM and CMs of all states. Prime Minister and Chief Ministers should work together as a team. Only when we work together as a team, we can make real progress. States must be involved in all decision making processes. State governments must be involved while sanctioning all major projects. It would be our priority to consider state governments as equal partners in the process of progress. When we talk of equal partnership, it reflects on our genuine intentions. If your intentions are right and genuine then having opposition parties ruling state governments will not be a hurdle.

NBT: Today, the people of this country are troubled by rising prices. Rising prices cannot be controlled without the help of state governments. How do we seek the cooperation of state governments in this case?

NM: It is necessary to remove the imbalance between demand and supply to control the runaway inflation and rising prices. For this, it is necessary to ensure supply of food grains and other produce in adequate quantity. This would be possible. Only when agriculture is given focused attention and irrigation schemes are strengthened. It is necessary to work with a new mindset to achieve this. Our election manifesto speaks of 'Prime Minister Irrigation Scheme' in addition to revolutionary reforms in the agriculture sector. Apart from this, today, no real time data is available in our agriculture sector with the result; it becomes a futile exercise to make plans for the development of agriculture sector. We must get real time data in this segment and then make policies and programmes based on it. We will create a special fund to stabilize the prices of food grains. We want to propagate the white revolution of Gujarat all over the country.

NBT: Today, all the hopes of the citizens of this country are pinned on you. Do you feel burdened with these? How have you prepared to prove yourself?

NM: As a matter of fact, with the deterioration in the level of politics in the last decade, it is natural that the common man has a feeling of frustration and hatred in his mind towards government machinery. After a long time peoples' interest in electoral politics has returned and we see the trust of the voters being reinstated. A wave of hope is sweeping the entire nation. I am fully aware that the entire nation has pinned a lot of hopes on BJP and I believe that the citizens too have a right to dream and be optimistic. They should be free to build hopes. There is nothing wrong in it. We are sensitive to these and we have mentally prepared ourselves to put in tremendous efforts to fulfill their aspirations.

NBT: It is not easy to recover black money which is deposited in foreign banks. Many international laws have become obstacles to recover this money. How will you remove these obstacles and if the black money is recovered, how will the common man of this country get benefitted? How much black money has been lying abroad?

NM: First and foremost is the intention and determination to get back black money. BJP has clearly expressed its intention to retrieve black money. We accept that the problem of black money is a major challenge. This is not only evasion of taxes but also anti-national tendency. Black money which has been generated and which is deposited overseas can also be used for an illegal and anti-national activities. For us, it is a very major issue. I would like to promise to the people of this nation that it is my personal commitment to get back the black money and we will form a task force immediately. We will also make necessary changes in the legal framework along with legal reforms. Not only this, we will get back such black money in the country and distribute a part of it to honest tax payers, particularly the salaried class. It is very essential that our tax system should encourage an honest tax payer, reward him and at the same time handle the tax evaders with an iron hand.

NBT: Now the Parliamentary elections are in the final stage. What is your guess on the emerging scenario of the next Parliament?

NM: Now the picture is very clear. People of the nation want a change. UPA government which is deeply stuck in the despicable issues like inflation, corruption and scandals has not made any contribution towards the progress of the nation. Polling has been completed in 8 out of 9 rounds and the voting pattern of these stages has made it clear that the voters have decided to throw UPA out of power. They have also laid the foundation for BJP and its alliances to form the government. Now, only 41 seats are remaining for which polling yet to take place, I am sure that voters will give strong support to BJP and allies in these constituencies too.'

NBT: You say that Congress cannot cross double digit figures, in which case who do you think would be the largest opposition party?

NB: Yes indeed! Congress is going to create a new record of poor performance in its entire history. It is very like that it will shrink to only a double digit number of seats. In such a situation, how the present leadership would make the party's presence relevant is hidden in the realms of future. We sincerely want that the largest opposition party, irrespective of which it is, should conduct themselves with positive approach and establish a tradition of responsible politics for the progress and welfare of the nation.

NBT: Do you think anyone is capable for the post of Prime Minister from Congress party? If yes, who is it?

NM: You see, I believe that Congress has become a leaderless party today. Congress does not have any capable leader who connects with the people, whose voice echoes from Kashmir to Kanyakumari. Devotion to Gandhi family is the only single point agenda of most Congressmen. In such a situation, selecting a Prime Ministerial candidate is a far cry. Right from the days of Indira Gandhi, the stature of any leader was not allowed to grow to any heights which later may prove to be a challenge to the Gandhi family.

NBT: How do you evaluate Dr. Manmohan Singh on a personal level? Is it that he could not prove his capabilities only as a Prime Minister or do you think that otherwise he does have many good qualities as an individual?

NM: To understand any individual and then evaluate him you should have known and studied him from close quarters. I have not got the opportunity to meet Dr Manmohan Singh on many occasions. Yes! I have met him a couple of times on official occasions but I do not think it will be appropriate and justified to form any opinion based on these very few occasions. As far as his performance as a Prime Minister is concerned, the country has understood the real state of affairs after seeing his dismal performance during his tenure.

NBT: If you come to power, which are those five tasks which you would like to perform immediately?

NM: Our first priority would be to restore faith of the people in Government and Government machinery. Second priority would be to take concrete steps to revive the economy. Third priority would be to take immediate steps to contain inflation and rising prices. Fourth priority would be to instil life into the Government machinery and to make decision making process fast and robust. The fifth priority would be getting rid of policy paralysis.

NBT: Do you think that somebody can create obstacles in your path to the post of Prime Minister?

NM: You see, a son from an ordinary family has reached this far. In this long social and political journey, I got the support, blessings and good wishes of innumerable people. I think this is an imaginary question and it has no relationship with the reality and truth.

NBT: Do you remember Vajpeyee ji? Will your Government have a reflection of his style of functioning?

NM: Being the soldier of BJP, I definitely keep remembering him. He has to his credit, the success of running of the only full term non-Congress government in the history of India. He did a lot of work by keeping in mind the interests of the common man and which is remembered even today. And since I have travelled a lot of distance in my political career under Vajpayee ji's patronage, I am a fan of his unique style of functioning and his intense eagerness to be always connected with people. His biggest achievement was the manner in which he provided relief to the public of this nation from the rising prices and inflation of the Congress regime. We want that the common public should get this relief once again.

Interview of BJP leader Narendra Modi with Reuters

July 12, 2013

Narendra Modi is a polarising figure, evoking visceral reactions across the political spectrum. Critics call him a dictator while supporters believe he could make India an Asian superpower.

Reuters spoke to Modi at his official Gandhinagar residence. In a rare interview, since he was appointed head of the BJP's election campaign in June.

Here are edited excerpts from the interview.

Question: Is it frustrating that many people still define you by 2002?

People have a right to be critics. We are a democratic country. Everyone has their own view. I would feel guilty if I did something wrong. Frustration comes when you think "I got caught. I was stealing and I got caught." That's not my case.

Question: Do you regret what happened?

I'll tell you. India's Supreme Court is considered a good court today in the world. The Supreme Court created a special investigative team (SIT) and top-most; very bright officers who overlook oversee the SIT. That report came. In that report, I was given a thoroughly clean chit. Another thing, any person if we are driving a car, we are a driver, and someone else is driving a car and we're sitting behind, even then if a puppy comes under the wheel, will it be painful or not? Of course it is. Whether I'm a chief minister or not, I'm a human being. If something bad happens anywhere, it is natural to be sad.

Question: Should your government have responded differently?

Up till now, we feel that we used our full strength to set out to do the right thing.

Question: But do you think you did the right thing in 2002?

Absolutely. Whatever brainpower the Supreme Being has given us, and the experience which I've got, and whatever I had available in that situation. This is what the SIT had also investigated.

Question: Do you believe India should have a secular leader?

We do believe that ... But what is the definition of secularism? For me, my secularism is, India first. I say, the philosophy of my party is 'Justice to all. Appeasement to none'. This is our secularism.

Question: Critics say you are an authoritarian, supporters say you are a decisive leader. Who is the real Modi?

If you call yourself a leader, then you have to be decisive. If you're decisive then you have the chance to be a leader. These are two sides to the same coin ... People want him to make decisions. Only then they accept the person as a leader. That is a quality, it's not a negative. The other thing is if someone was an authoritarian then how would he be able to run a government for so many years?

… Without a team effort how can you get success? And that's why I say Gujarat's success is not Modi's success. This is the success of Team Gujarat.

Question: What about the su ggestion that you don't take criticism?

I always say the strength of democracy lies in criticism. If there is no criticism that means there is no democracy. And if you want to grow, you must invite criticism. And I want to grow, I want to invite criticism. But I'm against allegations. There is a vast difference between criticism and allegations. For criticism, you have to research, you'll have to compare things, you'll have to come with data, factual information, and then you can criticize. Now no one is ready to do the hard work. So the simple way is to make allegations. In a democracy, allegations will never improve situations. So, I'm against allegations but I always welcome criticism.

On his popularity in opinion polls

I can say that since 2003, in however many polls have been done, people have selected me as the best chief minister. And as best chief minister, it wasn't just people from Gujarat who liked me, not like that. People outside of Gujarat have also voted like that for me. One time, I wrote a letter to the India Today Group's Aroon Purie. I requested him – "Every time I'm a winner, so next time please drop Gujarat, so that someone else gets a chance. Or else I'm just winning. Please keep me out of the competition. And besides me, give someone else a shot at it."

Question: Allies and people within the BJP say you are too polarizing a figure

In America, if there's no polarization between Democrats and Republicans, then how would democracy work? It's bound (to happen). In a democracy, there will be a polarization between Democrats and Republicans.

This is democracy's basic nature. It's the basic quality of democracy. If everyone moved in one direction, would you call that a democracy?

But allies and partners still find you controversial

Up till now, no one from my party or the people who are allied with us, I've never read nor heard any official statement (about this from them). It might have been written about in the media. They write in a democracy … and if you have any name that this person is there in the BJP who said this, then I can respond.

Question: How will you persuade minorities including Muslims to vote for you?

First thing, to Hindustan's citizens, to voters, Hindus and Muslims, I'm not in favour of dividing. I'm not in favour of dividing Hindus and Sikhs. I'm not in favour of dividing Hindus and Christians. All the citizens, all the voters, are my countrymen. So my basic philosophy is, I don't address this issue like this. And that is a danger to democracy also. Religion should not be an instrument in your democratic process.

Question: If you become PM, which leader would you emulate?

The first thing is, my life's philosophy and what I follow is: I never dream to become something. I always dream of doing something. So to be inspired by my role models, I don't need to become anything. If I want to learn something from Vajpayee, then I can just implement that in Gujarat. For that, I don't have to have dreams of (higher office in) Delhi. If I like something about Sardar Patel, then I can implement that in my state. If I like something about Gandhiji, then I can implement that. Without talking about the Prime Minister's seat, we can still discuss that, yes, from each one we have to learn the good things.

On the goals the next government should achieve

Look, whichever new government comes to power, that government's first goal will be to regain the confidence that has broken completely in people.

The government tries to push a policy. Will it continue that policy or not? In two months, if they face pressure, will they change it? Will they do something like — an event happens now and they'll change a decision from 2000? If you change decisions from the past, you will bring the policy back-effects. Who in the world will come here?

So whichever government comes to power, it would need to give people confidence, it should build the trust in people, "Yes, in policies there will be consistency", if they promise people something, they will honor that promise, they will fulfil. Then you can position yourself globally.

Question: People say economic development in Gujarat is hyped up?

In a democracy, who is the final judge? The final judge is the voter. If this was just hype, if this was all noise, then the public would see it everyday. "Modi said he would deliver water." But then he would say "Modi is lying. The water hasn't reached." Then why would he like Modi? In India's vibrant democracy system, and in the presence of vibrant political parties, if someone chooses him for the third time, and he gets close to a two-third majority then people feel what is being said is true. Yes, the road is being paved, yes, work is being done, and children are being educated. There are new things coming for health. 108 (emergency number) service is available. They see it all. So that's why someone might say hype or talk, but the public won't believe them. The public will reject it. And the public has a lot of strength, a lot.

Question: Should you be doing more for inclusive economic growth?

Gujarat is a state that people have a lot of expectations from. We're doing a good job, that's why the expectations are high. As they should be. Nothing is wrong.

Question: On indicators like malnutrition, infant mortality

Infant mortality has improved tremendously in Gujarat, tremendously. Compared to every other state in Hindustan, we are a better performing state. Second thing, malnutrition, in Hindustan today, real-time data is not available. When you don't have real time data, how are you going to analyse?

We do believe in inclusive growth, we do believe that the benefits of this development must reach to the last person and they must be the beneficiary. So this is what we're doing.

Question: People want to know who is the real Modi – Hindu nationalist leader or pro-business chief minister?

I'm nationalist. I'm patriotic. Nothing is wrong. I'm a born Hindu. Nothing is wrong. So, I'm a Hindu nationalist. You can say I'm a Hindu nationalist because I'm a born Hindu. I'm patriotic so nothing is wrong in it. As far as progressive, development-oriented, workaholic, whatever they say, this is what they are saying. So there's no contradiction between the two. It's one and the same image.

Question: On Brand Modi and people behind the PR strategy

The western world and India – there's a huge difference between them. Here, India is such a country that a PR agency will not be able to make a person into anything. Media can't make anything of a person. If someone tries to project a false face in India, then my country reacts badly to it. Here, people's thinking is different. People won't tolerate hypocrisy for very long. If you project yourself the way you actually are, then people will accept even your shortcomings. Man's weaknesses are accepted. And they'll say, yes, okay, he's genuine, he works hard. So our country's thinking is different. As far as a PR agency is concerned, I have never looked at or listened to or met a PR agency. Modi does not have a PR agency. Never have I kept one.

In a special conversation with Asian News International

In this interview, Modi revealed secrets of his successful use of social media. He talked about how social media could be used to its maximum potential for making India better. BJP's efforts are commendable and he was happy about it. Social media is a medium of expression of equal citizens which means that a single institution or individual cannot govern it nor can it be used recklessly for personal gains. It is based on established ethical norms of respecting the autonomy and freedom of others. This should be applicable to social media too. Social media promotes true emotions, genuine feelings and justified expectations for social transformation. We should listen to these feelings and also admire them, respect them. In a special interview with Asian News International, Chief Minister of Gujarat presented the uniqueness of this media to bring in awareness in the minds of the voters.

Question: Modi ji, there has been a lot of buzz in recent days on the use of Social Media by you as well as by the BJP as an organization. What role do you see Social Media playing in this campaign?

If one would recall, during one of my recent speeches I had observed that this is the Age of Knowledge and Information. No single individual or organization enjoys a monopoly on possession and dissemination of knowledge and information. It is imperative to listen and learn as much as pronounce, in this Digital age. Thus it becomes requisite for every Indian Leader to be able to have a two-way communication with the people, especially our Youth. Social Media to me is the most powerful channel for accomplishing this. I was recently in Pune to meet with the students of Fergusson College. I was pleasantly surprised over the seriousness with which Youth responded to my request through Social Media for ideas and suggestions for that speech. I am happy to note that the BJP as an organization is looking to creatively harness Social Media to crowd source ideas on how we can change and transform India for the better.

Question: Modi ji, could you share instances where you have been able to experience the power of Social Media the most?

It is important for us to expand our definition of what constitutes Social Media. To me it is not just about Twitter and Facebook. For instance, I am amazed at how YouTube as a medium of video sharing has made e-Learning accessible to so many people. Or when I look at an application like WhatsApp and how simple it is to use, one begins to appreciate the power of this medium. Often the first reports when a disaster strikes or an unfortunate incident happens are received via one of these Social Media channels. I see the real power of Social Media come through, during such moments of crisis. Recently during the Uttarakhand disaster I was pleasantly surprised at the positive role played by Social Media in bringing home news of the missing to their loved ones.

Question: Modi ji, many of your critics allege that you have massive PR machinery that manages your Social Media presence to carry out your propaganda. What would you say to them?

My humble request to everybody is to not insult and insinuate the common man, the youth of India, who have found a medium through which they are able to make their voice heard. It is important for us to understand the nature of this medium. It is a medium of equals. No single individual or organization can control it or manipulate it. We must respect this basic nature of this medium. Let me give you the example of a recent incident when a restaurant in Mumbai had to suffer due to rank intolerance of the Congress party. The Sales Receipt of that restaurant was shared on Social Media by some conscious citizens. It soon went viral. It came to the attention of one newspaper, which published a story on it. I merely added my voice to express solidarity on this issue, with all those venting their frustration and despair on it, through Social Media. This is the nature of the Medium. It is essentially about listening, sharing and dialogue.

Question: Modi ji, one of the biggest complaints of Social Media is what many people call "trolling". Abuse in Social Media has become a big problem. Recently there have been personal attacks on eminent people and their families. What is your suggestion on how to deal with this menace?

Our Culture is known for its long standing traditions of respecting our elders and our scholars. In the same vein, we worship and celebrate Women's Power as Shakti. Expressing one's opinion on Social Media, does not imply, that we abandon our Culture and value systems. Our conduct at home, offices and schools, is based on certain well appreciated norms of mutual respect and dignity. The same is to apply to our conduct on Social Media as well.

This is what I mean by the need for Modernization, and not Westernization. We must embrace modern technology and harness its Power. But our use of modern technology must not come at the expense of us forgetting our values and ethics.

What was the word you mentioned just now … ah yes "trolling"? It reminds me of how disinformation would be used by Nations against each other, by planting false stories and creating havoc during Wars. It is unfortunate that some vested interests are misusing the power of Social Media to indulge in a similar effort. Recently I had come across an instance where a morphed digital image was circulated with a malicious and slanderous intention. Technology makes it quite easy to accomplish this. We however, have to guard against this sort of disinformation, peddled through fake sites and fictitious accounts. We have to use our judgment on Social Media on what sources to trust just as we would do in real life where we are able to differentiate between genuine news and rumours.

Question: Modi ji, there is a lot of debate on how representative Social Media is representing India's realities. How seriously should we take Social Media? How many of these individuals on Social Media will actually vote?

You would recall in a recent speech I had alluded to the need for Electoral Reforms like Online Voting and the option to reject Candidates. We have to ensure our Youth stays engaged in our Democratic process. We have to make our Democratic process accessible to them through a medium, which they use and comprehend the most. Social Media in my opinion is a tool that can help in this. I can tell you there are real voices, serious voices that want to be heard. For instance, my request for ideas and suggestions on the problems of our Education System elicited serious response. Similarly, solicitation of ideas towards my upcoming speech in Hyderabad has brought forth responses on the state of the economy, jobs, roadmap for Andhra Pradesh and much more. There is real sentiment out there, full of veritable emotions and legitimate aspirations to do something, to make a difference. We have to listen, appreciate and respect that sentiment, which is being expressed through Social Media. Today scores of Indians have mobile phones. Even a simple thought expressed through the mode of a SMS can travel far and wide, in a matter of minutes, through multiple sharing. We must harness all possibilities that are out there in the public domain.

Elections and campaigns will come and go, however, our mission to make our Democracy, more deliberative, and consequently purposeful should remain uncompromised. It should be responsive to our Youth, who today constitute a significant part of the population.

Excerpts of his interview with editor of *Amar Ujala*, a Hindi daily

In an e-mail interview with Ashutosh Chaturvedi and Sanjay Pandey of *'Amar Ujala'*- a Hindi daily, Modi said that if the conscience is clear then even the most difficult task can be accomplished. He believes that for the development and progress of the nation, each state must have its own model for its progress befitting its individual needs. Here is the detailed interview:

Question: China has always been creating problems for India. What would be your strategy for China?

Answer: Our Government will be committed to the security of our borders but if there are any disputes related to boundaries, we believe in sitting across the table like matured and responsible neighbours and finding a peaceful solution. Neither do we want to threaten anyone nor do we want that they should threat us. We desire that we should look eye to eye and discuss.

Question: Your relations with USA have been making not only national but international headlines. In which direction would our relations with USA move?

Answer: When we want to talk of two countries, personal loss or personal experience assume secondary importance. My thoughts on this subject are very clear. Whether it is USA or any other country, we are committed to establish friendly ties as a responsible nation. During Vajpayee's tenure, Indo-US ties had made a new beginning. We will work towards taking it further ahead.

Question: If you become the Prime Minister, what would be your priority? What will be the role of senior leaders like Advani, Joshi in the proposed Govt?

Answer: After forming the Govt, our first task will be to reinstate the faith of people in the Govt and its machinery. Secondly, we will take effective steps to revive the economy. Immediate steps will be taken to contain inflation. We will have to revive the Govt machinery and make it robust. Apart from this, it will be our priority to get rid of 'Policy Paralysis'. The question of the role of senior leaders will arise after the Govt is formed, we will take a decision at an appropriate time.

Question: It is said that you have created enmity with all the regional parties; be it Jayalalita or Mamata or Mayawati. If you need their support, how will you manage?

Answer: Allegations and counter-allegations are common during elections. This also happens to be the unique feature of our democracy. I am very confident that an NDA Government is going to be formed with the leadership and majority of BJP. NDA with BJP and its allies will certainly achieve the necessary number of seats for forming the Govt. We have a very strong and big alliance of 25 parties and this also probably happens to be largest pre-poll alliance in the history of Indian elections.

Question: What is your opinion about Gandhi family? You always target Rahul and Sonia but hardly speak about Priyanka whereas she never loses any opportunity to speak against you. What is your comment on this?

Answer: I have already said that she has full right to canvass for her mother and brother. It is natural that a daughter will always defend her mother and as sister would be protective about her brother. I do not have any problem with this.

Question: Robert Vadra is also targeted by you. Uma Bharati says that when NDA forms the Govt, Vadra will be

behind bars. Will you institute any enquiry to investigate the charges of alleged corruption against him?

Answer: You must understand that the country is governed by the rule of the land. It is not run on the likes and dislikes of the people holding high positions. Nobody is above the law of the land and that includes me. Therefore, this cannot be a point of discussion.

Question: During his discussions with Amar Ujala, Ahmed Patel has said that Narendra Modi cannot be called as anybody's friend. What is your reaction to this?

Answer: It is my clear opinion that you can have competition in Politics but not enmity. Some political compulsion must have made him give such a statement but if has really given such a statement, I can only say that I am happy with my friendship and may he be happy with his enmity.

Question: Rising prices and inflation has destroyed the common man and you have announced in your speeches that you will control inflation. How are you going to do it?

Answer: To control rising prices, it is necessary to end the imbalance between demand and supply. For this, we will have to regulate the food grain laws and also ensure availability of other supplements in sufficient quantity. This will be possible only when emphasis is given to agriculture and irrigation schemes are developed. We need to work with a new way of thinking. We have mentioned the Prime Minister Agricultural Irrigation Scheme in our election manifesto to bring about a revolutionary change in the field of agriculture. It is surprising that we do not have any real time data in the field of agriculture. This means that we do not have any robust basis to start new plans and projects in the field of agriculture. We will obtain real time data in the field of agriculture and formulate our policies and programmes on its basis. We will create a special fund to regulate the prices of food grains. We would also like to spread the white revolution, so successful in Gujarat, all over the country.

Question: What is your opinion about FDI? Is it necessary for the economic development of India? What is your take on FDI in retail sector?

Answer: Accelerated progress is necessary for the revival of economy and investment is necessary for progress. We can expect investment only when the climate is favourable. We can expect investment only when we are able to restore the confidence of the investors in our system. Policies definitely have their own importance but credibility and track record also mean a lot. We have clarified our stand on FDI in the manifesto of the party.

Question: In spite having great leaders in UP and Bihar from time to time, these states are continue to be backward. How can the conditions in these states be improved?

Answer: Generally the problems of the all the people of this country are similar but the population of UP and Bihar had to face the brunt of the parties who spread communal feelings. Instead of promoting the politics of development, these states were left far behind as a result of political rivalries. This is the reason that these states which gave stalwarts to the nation are in a deplorable state. I feel that our country cannot be on a path of development as a whole unless these two states do not lead the way. The people, particularly the youth of UP and Bihar are very enthusiastic about BJP and they have many hopes from us. If we come to power, we will prepare a special roadmap for the development of these states. It is a matter of intentions. If your intentions are genuine, there are tremendous possibilities of making these states also progressive. These states, so rich in natural resources are deprived of development and progress only because of corruption and bad administration. In fact, it is now clear that the people of these two states are also equally keen for progress and good administration as the people of other states are. Therefore, it will be our endeavor to work hard to fulfill the ambitions of these people.

Question: How many seats will BJP win in UP? Who do you think is your main competitor in UP?

Answer: BJP is going to register a massive win with a very large margin. Congress is not at all in the race. At the same time, people

of UP have understood the opportunistic policies of Samajwadi Party and Bahujan Samaj Party. The hunger for progress is all the more evident in the largest state of the country. The massive turnout in BJP's rallies is a testimony to the fact that the contest in the state is going to be one sided and in favour of BJP. Citizens of the state who are fed up with the politics of communalism and casteism are going to endorse the progressive policies of BJP. This time .our performance in UP will be an all-time best. I have publicly said many times, 'Everyone is going to be washed off in UP this time which means SP, BSP and Congress'.

Question: If you win a seat, both in Vadodara and Varanasi, which seat will you surrender?

Answer: My party will decide which constituency I will represent in the Parliament. Being a disciplined party worker, I am committed to accept the decision of my party with complete dedication.

Question: It is the talk of the town in Varanasi that as soon as Modi is elected as their representative, there will be a sea change in Varanasi. You have aroused tremendous expectations in the minds of the voters. How will you fulfill them?

Answer: I will implement a special plan to bring back the old glory to this cultural and spiritual capital of the country. We want to see Varanasi as a world heritage city. It is my ambition to make this city of knowledge, philosophy, meditation and culture as a global tourism centre. Ganga is the lifeline of Varanasi and it has the pace of mother in our culture. But the bureaucratic indifference has made the river one of the most polluted. While it is claimed that millions of rupees are being spent on cleaning projects, facts show that under the disguise of cleaning the river, there has been only rampant corruption. Our Government will carry out the work of purification of Ganga with complete dedication and will ensure that the faith of millions of devotee is not betrayed. The weavers of Varanasi are an integral part of its history. Banarasi sari is famous not only in India but all over the world. This glorious legacy of generations together had to suffer at the hands of the Govts at Delhi and Lucknow because of their insensitivity. I am determined to modernise the handlooms and to do value addition to this industry. We will ensure that right from raw material stage, manufacturing and marketing we will establish proper mechanism so that the Banarasi sari regains its lost glory. Banaras which was famous as a seat of knowledge throughout the world, which even today attracts tourists from all over the world, today has a very pathetic story to tell. It is sheer negligence and ignorance of our governments that this town which has tourists' presence in such large numbers from all over the world is deprived of basic facilities. We will make sure that the city in provided with all basic necessities. We will build world class facilities in terms of roads, electricity, water, transport and hospitality to welcome our guests from all over the world. We want that the tourists should return with many pleasant memories of their stay.

Question: When you filed your nomination, you gave a very emotional statement, "I don't think anyone has sent me here nor have I come here. Like a child going to his Mother, I have come here to Ganga. I want to serve this land." You are fully aware of the condition of Ganga in UP including Banaras. "How will you purify and salvage Ganga?"

Answer: No task is bigger than your will-power. If you have the genuine intention to work with faith and genuine determination, you can achieve it. As far as Ganga is concerned, other than making very large plans on paper, nothing concrete has been done so far. The Central Govt squandered millions of rupees under the name of cleaning Ganga but it continues to be dirty. I want to give you the example of Gujarat here; there was a time when Sabarmati River has turned into a dirty canal. Nothing was left which could be called a river. It had become a dry and barren basin. The garbage of the city was dumped in the river in many places. We took up the movement of cleaning this river which was passing through the city. Under the Scheme of joining the rivers, we flooded it with the water from Narmada and gave it the look of a beautiful river. Today, Sabarmati River has become a place of recreation for the citizens. Not only has it added to the beauty of the city, since it is flooded with water throughout the year the water level of the city has also increased. All I want to emphasize is that with the limited resources at state level, we have been able to transform a river which had lost its original look and glory. It is obvious that the cleansing of Ganga will have to be taken up on similar lines. The scale is going to be definitely very large but it's all a question of intentions and sincerity. To emancipate Ganga which is so close to the heart and faith of millions of the citizens, we implement this robust plan with all seriousness.

Question: During your election campaign, you travelled all over the country and that includes UP too where you held rallies in most of the major cities. Today, peoples' expectations are at peak. How will you salvage the entire UP?

Answer: The deteriorating standard of politics during the last few years has generated a feeling of hatred and frustration towards the Government in the minds of people. After a long time, a lot of interest has been generated in the minds of the people regarding election politics. A wave of hope is sweeping the entire nation. I am fully aware that people have a lot of hopes from BJP. I appreciate that our people also have a right to rekindle the lamp of hopes and aspirations which are close to their hearts. There is nothing wrong to have your expectations at the peak. We are fully aware of this and we are also mentally prepared to put in commensurate efforts. Development of Uttar Pradesh is our priority. With the development of this state, we will get a lot of help in removing the imbalance between Western and Eastern India.

Question: How can the Central Government elevate the condition of any state without the cooperation of state government?

Answer: It is true that the path of progress gets easier if there is cooperation between Centre and State. Involvement of both the sides at the time of formulating and implementation of policies takes the level of performance to a new peak. We will work hard to establish cordial relations between Centre and State. We will try to get a public consensus on disputable issues. We will be continuously engaged in creating a great India in the interest of the country.

Question: During your election campaign in Uttarakhand, you had said that the calamity in Uttarakhand has shaken you up but I did not get the permission to go there and wipe the

tears of the affected people? What model do you have now for the development of Uttarakhand?

Answer: We understand the unique, special needs and problems of all the hilly and far-flung states. We will create a Development priorities model which is based on the advice of the Governments of these states so that peoples' expectations are fulfilled. BJP is committed to mobilise energies at the global level for the protection and preservation of ecology of Himalayas. We will take many unprecedented and innovative steps like creating synergy between various regions and areas, inter-government partnership, by starting a wonderful and unique programme like 'National Mission on Himalaya'. We will also start Himalaya Protection fund, and going to establish Central Technology Institution particularly devoted for Himalayan Technology. We will implement a special project particularly to prevent melting of Himalayan glaciers (from where most of the rivers of India originate). BJP will study the major problems and challenges of Uttarakhand and will take steps in the direction of the progress of the state.

Question: You have focused on Tourism industry. You have said that there are enormous opportunities for tourism in Himachal. You are emotionally and personally associated with Himachal. How will you make inroads in the inaccessible hills of Himachal?

Answer: Tourism always play a definite and important role in the economy of the world. There are enormous opportunities for tourism in our country too but unfortunately we have not been able to tap these so far to the full extent. Himachal, which can attract the tourists, has all the ingredients for tourism industry. All it needs is efforts from the Government to work in that direction. We will prepare a plan to develop tourism in Himachal by keeping in mind the realities of the local conditions. Our country has a rich legacy of spiritualism and philosophy. Himachal has the possibility of attracting the followers of Buddhism from all over the world. It is necessary to understand that infrastructure is considered as a prerequisite for development of tourism industry. Primary needs like roads, electricity, water and transportation facilitate the tourist. We will try to create the necessary infrastructure in Himachal to promote tourism industry.

Question: Kashmir is one of the biggest challenge to the country. How will you manage this?

Answer: Kashmir is an integral part of India. I have every reason to believe that the Citizens of Kashmir have an equal faith in the constitution of India as the people from other states have. In this way, all the rights given by the Constitution of India are available to them also. The problem of Kashmir has been a big challenge to the country. In the present condition, we have to work on two issues. First- we must win the heart of people of Kashmir. We must win their confidence too. We must assure the Kashmiris, who have been living in a confused state from mind right from the beginning that the entire country is with them. We will work with honest intentions for their progress, peace and comfort. Second- we have to bridge the gap of mistrust. We will put in sincere and genuine efforts to remove the sense of mistrust in the minds of Kashmiri brethren. In this effort, we will make sure that they experience good administration and also make them a partner in progress. We will take special steps to eradicate wide-spread unemployment in the state. Apart from this, the party has a desire to take trade and tourism industry in the state to a different height. To sum up, we will make all possible efforts to tread the path of Kashmiriyat (Spirit of Kashmir), Jamhooriayat (Patriotism) and Insaniyat (Humanitarianism) to really make it the heaven on earth.

Question: Pakistan has been consistently defying and challenging India but it is also true that we cannot change our neighbour, how will you manage Pakistan?

Answer: I have made it clear in the past too that I believe in the principle of 'Vasudhaiva Kutumbakam; the entire world is one large family. The relationship between two nations should be based on mutual respect and co-existence. India and Pakistan are inheritors of a common history and legacy. Both are struggling with the problem of poverty. The result is that poverty has led to problems like illiteracy, improper health care with which both countries are struggling. I feel that instead of fighting with each other, it is better, for both the nations, to fight with poverty.

Plans for the nation

Narendra Modi has prepared a master plan for the development and progress of the nation which probably cannot be implemented completely with immediate effect but which has set targets and if it is taken seriously, it can certainly be implemented. It is not easy to eradicate chronic maladies like corruption and inflation which are affecting our progress but the entire nation is looking at him with a sense of positive anticipation and are eager to learn about the fundamental difference in his approach which will change the direction of nation's march. BJP's election manifesto is a challenge for Modi because its implementation is an uphill task. BJP was late in declaring its manifesto. It was said that Modi's wishes had to be incorporated in the manifesto and hence there was a delay. We are reproducing the election manifesto of BJP, verbatim. Nothing has been added/subtracted by the author in the manifesto.

"I want to make three promises. First, I will not hesitate to make any efforts to fulfill any responsibility that the people of the country put on my shoulders. Second, I will not do anything for my personal benefit and three I will not work with any malafide intentions. I assure you of these three things."

-Narendra Modi

The election manifesto has reached the voters with these covering remarks from Narendra Modi. The election manifesto has been written by the Committee President Dr. Murali Manohar Joshi in which he says that India has been blessed with rare capabilities, democracy, demography and demand. If we make use of these with efficiency and capability, then we can reach great heights and India is capable of scaling these heights. One of the reasons for these deplorable conditions has been our malafide intentions which have ruled this country for the last six decades and we will show how different we are in this aspect. The policies and action plans of BJP will have only one goal- a great Bharat. Its roadmap will be everyone's participation, everyone's progress. This is our commitment to the nation and its citizens.

Election Manifesto

Our pledge
Ek Bharat - Shreshtha Bharat
Vibrant and Participatory Democracy
Empowered and Inspired People
Inclusive and Sustainable Development
Quality life in Villages and Cities
Basic Amenities to All
Flourishing Agriculture
Productive Youth
Involved Women
Robust physical and social Infrastructure
Innovative and Technologically driven Society
Globally competitive Economy
Brand India built on Quality
Strong, Effective and Futuristic Institutions
Open, Transparent and Systems-based Government
Pro-active, Pro-people Good Governance
To build a Modern India: the best foundation is our own Culture;
The best tool our own hands; and the best material our own aspirations

Preface

India is the most ancient civilization of the world and has always been looked upon by the world as a land of wealth and wisdom. India has been credited to have developed, apart from philosophy and mathematics, science and technology of a very high order, which had attracted scholars from all over the world. Al-Andalusi, a Spanish scholar in the 11th Century, in his monumental work 'Tabaqat al- Umam' had discussed the state of science in different countries. He writes, "The first nation to have cultivated science is India... India is known for wisdom of its people. Over many centuries all the kings of the past have recognized the ability of Indians in all branches of knowledge." Andalusi further states, "Indians, as known to all nations for many centuries, are the metal (essence) of wisdom, the source of fairness and objectivity. They are the people of sublime pensiveness, universal apologues, and useful and rare inventions."

India's contribution to the march of civilization goes back to several thousand years before the Christian era. From the Vedas to Upanishads and Gautam - the Buddha and Mahavira - the 24th Jain Tirthankara and then to Kautilya and Chandra Gupta and down up to the eighteenth century, India was respected for its flourishing economy, trade, commerce and culture. It had an international outreach from Korea to Arabia, from Bamiyan to Borobudur and beyond. Before the advent of Britishers, Indian goods were internationally recognized for their quality and craftsmanship. India had a much bigger role and presence in industry and manufacturing than any nation in Europe or Asia. It had a well-developed banking system and equally renowned businessmen, along with its financiers, who were contributing to create a flourishing and progressive economy. According to Sunderland, India was also one of the greatest shipbuilding nations and consequently had an access to international markets. Indian prosperity held the world in thrall. It was this wealth which attracted the foreigners - from Alexander to the Britishers.

Historical records establish the level of progress and prosperity attained by India before the advent of the Europeans. Indian advancement in mathematics, astronomy, physics and chemistry along with the biological sciences has been well recognized. India was a land of abundance, prosperity, affluence, a land of sharing and caring living in perfect harmony and peace with the nature. From ancient times almost all religions practiced in different parts of the world, have existed peacefully in India and will continue to do so. India thus provides the most ennobling experience in spiritual co-existence.

BJP recognizes that no nation could chart out its domestic or foreign policies unless it has a clear understanding about itself, its

history, its roots, its strengths and failings. In a highly mobile and globalized world, it is imperative for a nation to know its roots that provide sustenance to its people. \

Indian freedom struggle, which was inspired by Tilak, Gandhi, Aurobindo, Patel, Bose and others, had a clear vision of the civilizational consciousness of India. These leaders had directed the freedom movement, keeping the Indian ways and thoughts in the centre of their action. They had a vision to reconstruct the political and economic institutions of India as a continuum of civilizational consciousness, which made India one country, one people, and one Nation.

After achieving independence, the leaders at the helm of affairs lost the spirit and the vision, which the freedom movement had evoked. They discarded the vision and adopted the institutional framework of administration created by the Britishers which was quite alien to India's world-view. It is unfortunate that these leaders could not comprehend India's inner vitality, which was the main force responsible for India's survival despite several attacks and prolonged foreign rule and thus, failed to rekindle the spirit of India.

Even after nearly seven decades of our independence, the country has not been able to discover its innate vitality, the sense of time and the will to act. As a result, in spite of being the oldest civilization and a young republic, we are engulfed by a multi-dimensional crisis. A crisis, which has encompassed all walks of life. The rising disparities, division of social and communal base and terrorism leading to a fractured society is worsening the situation rapidly. The present crisis is the result of this confusion and disconnect from the seekings and sensibilities of the people. This is worse confounded by the weak and spineless leadership of the UPA Government. The tragedy is further raised up by their failure to diagnose the malady and find the remedy. Instead of creating a socio-economic and political paradigm of governance drawn from the civilizational consciousness of India, the leaders tried to follow whatever was being practiced in this or that western country.

Thus, we have wasted more than half of a century. Many other countries, even with smaller size and lesser resources, have surpassed us in development parameters. Another reason for this is that the Governance in these decades was marred by lack of trust, leading to excessive controls. It was also marked by lack of openness in Government and lack of people's participation. This has led to concentration of power in a few hands and lack of transparency breeding corruption and nepotism on a massive scale. The so-called 'liberalization' came in 1990s, but it was half-hearted. It didn't work because the rest of the eco-system remained the same. However, the beginning of the 21st century showed some light under the NDA rule. India started being reckoned as an economic superpower. The six-year rule of NDA had given the Nation many firsts, building an image in the International community. However, many of the hopes, potentials and projects have not been fully realized in the subsequent years. But after 2004, UPA came into power and the situation started worsening again. We missed a historic national opportunity once more.

UPA's biggest blow to the Indian political system is that they have taken out Genuineness from Governance; Authenticity from Administration. UPA has shown Governance of Enactment, not Action. It has given an Administration of Entitlement without delivery. We have become a polity of Promises, and not Performance. We represent an economy of deficits, a work culture of delays and an asset base of Deficiency. Worse, Congress-led UPA has made India a global synonym of Corruption, Scandal and Stagnation. To make it even worse, today, we are passing through total Decision and Policy Paralysis. Sluggish economic growth, unprecedented price rise and unstable Currency are its most visible facets.

The following demand urgent solutions; economy including agriculture, energy, environment including natural resources, education and health, employment, external and internal threats to security, empowerment, Governance, and erosion of moral and societal values.

If India has to survive as a nation, which it has to, in order to play its destined role in the comity of nations, if it has to make its voice heard for creating a peaceful and egalitarian world order, then we must take up the challenges with urgency and determination and provide proper solutions for them. It is a pity that we have a demoralized leadership presiding over the state apparatus, which is incompetent to handle the present problems. What is needed today is to arrive at a consensus about the 'Idea' of India and also to think and redesign our approach in consonance with the seekings and preferences of the Indian people.

The situation in the country is deteriorating rapidly. Delay in resolving the crisis would be dangerous. What is needed is to take lessons from history, recognise the vitality and resilience of India, the power of its world-view and utilize its strength, which drove it to glorious heights and analyse its weaknesses, which led to this abysmal fall. Pick up the thread from the point where the continuum of our civilizational consciousness was lost and reorient the polity in consonance with those strong points of Indian psyche which will be the engine for our future glory. Let's keep the windows open, have a clear understanding of the global scenario and how without destroying our uniqueness we can assimilate the best of the technological advancements.

We can achieve this goal provided the leaders seriously set to this task. What we need is a political party committed to deliver and a leadership with strong determination and political will. As Vivekananda had said, "All power is within you. You can do anything. Believe in that." Yes, the power lies in the people of India, in the inner sanctum sanctorum of Mother India. What is needed is to ignite the spark and Mother India would rise in her full glory.

As Sri Ma had once said that India had become the symbolic representation of all the difficulties of modern mankind but India will also be the land of its resurrection to a higher and truer life. The BJP will leave no stone unturned to fulfil the dream of 1.22 billion Indians.

Today, India is blessed with the rare capacity and opportunity of Democracy, Demography and Demand. If we are able to consolidate and harness them, we will be able to reach the heights which India deserves. The biggest reason for a sorry state of affairs is bad intentions on the part of those who have ruled the country for sixty years. And that is where we would show the first difference. For BJP, the goal of the policies and practices would be: Ek Bharat, Shreshtha Bharat! The path would be: Sabka Saath, Sabka Vikas. This is our commitment to the Nation and to the People.

With this determination of the party under the charismatic leadership of Shri Narendra Modi, we enter the elections to the 16th Lok Sabha and would work whole-heartedly to give a stable, strong, visionary and progressive Government to India.

It is an opportunity to change our fate and of our nation. Glory to Mother India, glory to Her children.

March 26, 2014 — Dr. (Prof.) Murali Manohar Joshi,
Chairman,
Manifesto Committee -2014

Attend the Imminent Present Challenges

Decade under the UPA - I and II can rightly be summed in one line, the 'Decade of Decay', in which India had a free fall on all fronts - be it governance, economy, diplomacy, foreign policy, border safety, etc. At the same time, corruption, scams and crime against women have reached to unacceptable levels. There has been gross misuse and total denigration of government and institutions. There has also been erosion of authority of the office of the Prime Minister. The Government dithered by each passing day, casting gloom and doom on the country that was once under the NDA regime called the 'Emerging Superpower'. In 2004, NDA left the Government with a near double digit growth. The Congress- led UPA could not even maintain that growth and mismanaged the country so badly that the growth rate declined to 4.8%, resulting the country falling in a deep mess. We have lost a wonderful opportunity and have pushed the country 20 years behind and rendered millions of men and women jobless.

Critical and urgent challenges facing the nation have been left unaddressed. Beyond impacting the immediate short-term, this is corroding the long-term potential of the nation. People feel frustrated and have lost hope in the system. Things must change and they must change now. BJP will take immediate and decisive action to address these issues on a priority basis.

Price Rise

Runaway food inflation has crippled household budgets and contributed to the overall inflationary trend under the Congress-led UPA's watch. Even worse, the food and nutritional security of millions is threatened. However, the Congress-led UPA government has remained insensitive and indifferent to the plight of the people; tying itself into knots with short-term, mis-directed steps. The committee of Chief Ministers, headed by Shri Narendra Modi, has already submitted a report on food inflation in 2011. The report was unfortunately not acted upon by the Congress-led UPA Government.

The BJP-led NDA Government's record of holding the prices is a demonstration of our commitment to break the vicious cycle of high inflation and high interest rates. Our immediate task will be to rein in inflation by several steps, such as:

- Put in place strict measures and special Courts to stop hoarding and black marketing.
- Setting up a Price Stabilisation Fund.
- Unbundle FCI operations into procurement, storage and distribution for greater efficiency.
- Leverage on technology to disseminate Real time data, especially to farmers - on production, prices, imports, stocks and overall availability.
- Evolve a single 'National Agriculture Market'.
- Promote and support area specific crops and vegetables linked to food habits of the people.

Employment and Entrepreneurship

The country has been dragged through 10 years of Jobless Growth by the Congress-led UPA Government. Under the broader economic revival, BJP will accord high priority to job creation and opportunities for entrepreneurship. We will:

- Strategically develop high impact domains like Labour-intensive manufacturing (viz. textile, footwear, electronics assembly, etc.) and Tourism.
- Strengthen the traditional employment bases of agriculture and allied industries, and retail - through modernization as well as stronger credit and market linkages.
- Harness the opportunities provided by the upgradation of infrastructure and housing for its job generating potential.

- Encourage and empower our youth for self-employment - incubating entrepreneurship as well as facilitating credit.

- Address the employability issue by initiating a multi-skills development programme in mission mode. Focus will be on job creation and entrepreneurship, in both rural and urban areas.

- Transform our Employment Exchanges into Career Centres - connecting our youth with job opportunities in a transparent and effective manner through the use of technology; as well as providing counselling and training.

Corruption

Corruption is a manifestation of poor Governance. Moreover, it reflects the bad intentions of those sitting in power. All pervasive corruption under the Congress-led UPA has become a 'National Crisis'.

We will establish a system, which eliminates the scope for corruption. We will do this through:

- Public awareness

- Technology enabled e-Governance - minimizing the discretion in the citizen-government interface.

- System-based, policy-driven governance - making it transparent.

- Rationalization and simplification of the tax regime - which is currently repulsive for honest tax payers.

- Simplification of the processes and procedures at all levels - bestowing faith in the citizens, institutions and establishments.

Black Money

By minimizing the scope for corruption, we will ensure minimization of the generation of black money. BJP is committed to initiate the process of tracking down and bringing back black money stashed in foreign banks and offshore accounts. We will set up a Task Force for this purpose and to recommend amendments to existing laws or enact new laws. The process of bringing back black money to India what belongs to India will be put in motion on priority. We will also proactively engage with foreign Governments to facilitate information sharing on black money.

Decision and Policy Paralysis

The country has suffered a decade of maladministration and scams in addition to decision and policy paralysis; thus bringing growth and development to a grinding halt leading to a 'Governance deficit'. This situation will be changed and the engine of Government will be ignited again with strong willpower and commitment to public interest. We will also encourage the bureaucracy to take right decisions and contribute their might in building a modern India.

Poor Delivery

Wherever we go, we encounter bottlenecks. We experience it on a daily basis - in government offices for even the simplest of public services, in our courts buried in high pendency and so on. Similarly, we are known by a culture of missing links and lack of last mile connectivity. We have water but no pipeline to carry it; we have schools but no teachers; we have computers and machines but no electricity; we have scientists but no labs; we have instruments but no one to work on them. This reduces the pace of our performance and results into wastage of time, money and energy. Intent to do the right thing and the will to do things rightly is missing. This has to be attended to on a priority basis.

Whatever we do and provide for, the whole chain has to be kept in mind. With this in mind, we will:

- Remove bottlenecks and missing links in all sectors, activities and services.
- Focus on proper planning and execution for right outcomes.
- Strive for scale and speed with futuristic vision.
- Build institutions for today and tomorrow.

Credibility Crisis

The biggest challenge that India faces today is to restore the credibility of, and trust in the Union Government. In recent years, the Union Government has lost every semblance of credibility. Its intentions, integrity and initiatives, all are questionable. The Congress party has not only lowered the dignity of the Government, but also the dignity of India. This is what is driving recent adversities like the falling rupee and countries riding roughshod over us. The BJP will work for restoring the trust and credibility of the Government. We will also ensure that the chain of responsibility and accountability is built in the system.

Team India

Centre-State Relations

Strengthen the Framework

India is a diverse country. Diverse communities settled in vastly different regions have their own aspirations. Taking these aspirations into consideration, the centre and the states therefore have to evolve a working system, which leads to harmonious relations. The genuine grievances of every state will be addressed in a comprehensive manner.

- We will place Centre-State relations on an even keel through the process of consultation and strive for harmonious Centre-State relations.

- Our Government will be an enabler and facilitator in the rapid progress of states. We will evolve a model of national development, which is driven by the states.

- Team India shall not be limited to the Prime Minister led team sitting in Delhi, but will also include Chief Ministers and other functionaries as equal partners.

- Ensure fiscal autonomy of States while urging financial discipline.

- Create 'Regional Councils of States', with common problems and concerns, with a view to seeking solutions that are applicable across a group of states.

- We will encourage cooperation among states on security-related issues, inter-state disputes and for removing inter-regional economic disparities and promoting tourism.

- We recognize the special needs and unique problems of the hill and desert states. In consultation with the Governments of these states, state-specific developmental priorities/ models will be evolved so that the aspirations of the people are met.

- Given the unique status of Union Territories (UTs), they will receive special attention. We will focus on developing and strengthening the economy of UTs. Tourism will be promoted, tribal welfare and their rights will receive full attention, and infrastructure and coastal area development will be given top priority.

- We reiterate our commitment to the protection and integrated development of our island territories.

- The moribund forums like 'National Development Council' and 'Inter-State Council' will be revived and made into active bodies.

- Involve the state Governments in the promotion of foreign trade and commerce.

- Help the states mobilize resources through investments in industry, agriculture and infrastructure.

Integrating the Nation - Its Vastness and Voices

In a democracy, everyone is not only free, but also encouraged to voice his or her concerns. It is also necessary that these voices be heard and concerns redressed. However, all this should happen within the framework of our constitution and with the spirit of 'India First'. We have to keep the Nation at the forefront of our thoughts and actions. Any activity, which disrupts the integrity of the nation, cannot be in the interest of any segment of the society or any region of the country. All Indians living in different regions of the country have an equal stake in the progress of the country and they have to be assured of the fruits of the progress.

- Presently, we see that there is a vast regional disparity between different regions of the country along developmental parameters, particularly between the western part and the eastern part. Despite their richness in both natural as well as human resources, eastern part of India still lags behind.

- We shall give the highest priority towards bringing the eastern parts of the country on par with the western parts. To that extent, there shall be special focus and emphasis on the development of the eastern side of India.

- Government will play the role of an enabler and a facilitator to the rapid progress of the states; planning along regional aspirations, strengths and potentials, evolving appropriate strategies for various zones of the country - hilly regions, plains, desert and coastal areas.

Regional aspirations: BJP has always stood for greater decentralization through smaller States.

Northeast: Resource rich North-Eastern states are lagging behind in development due to poor governance, systemic corruption and poor delivery of public services. NDA government had initiated concrete steps to address the issue of development of Northeast by setting up the Ministry of North- Eastern Region. We will empower this Ministry with a broader charter and non-lapsable funds for the rapid development of the region.

BJP will:

-Put special emphasis on enhancing the connectivity within the region and to the rest of the country.

-There will be special emphasis on massive infrastructure development, especially along the Line of Actual Control in Arunachal Pradesh and Sikkim.

- Address the issue of Flood control in Assam and river water management.

- Nurture more job generating opportunities like tourism and IT industry.

- Address the issue of infiltration and illegal immigrants in the Northeast region on a priority basis.

-This will include clear policy directions and effective control at the ground level.

- Complete all pending fencing work along the India-Bangladesh and India-Myanmar border, stepping up border security.

- Take measures for the safety of North-Eastern students studying across the country including setting up Hostels for North-Eastern students at various educational centres.

- Deal with Insurgent groups with a firm hand.

Jammu and Kashmir: Jammu and Kashmir was, is and shall remain an integral part of the Union of India. The territorial integrity of India is inviolable. BJP will pursue an agenda of equal and rapid development in all the three regions of the state - Jammu, Kashmir and Ladakh.

- The return of Kashmiri Pandits to the land of their ancestors with full dignity, security and assured livelihood will figure high on the BJP's agenda.

- The long pending problems and demands of refugees from Pakistan Occupied Kashmir (POK) will be addressed.

- BJP reiterates its stand on the Article 370, and will discuss this with all stakeholders and remains committed to the abrogation of this article.

- All steps will be taken to provide good governance, better infrastructure, educational opportunities, healthcare and more job opportunities, leading to a better quality of life in the valley.

Seemandhra and Telangana: BJP is committed to do full justice to Seemandhra, and address the issues of development and governance of Seemandhra and Telangana.

Decentralization and People's Participation From Representative to Participatory Democracy

India is a country of immense diversity - a highly decentralized federal structure is thus crucial in meeting the varied ideas and aspirations of our diverse people. Power is currently concentrated in Delhi and the State capitals. We believe this power should be genuinely decentralized. BJP has stood for greater decentralization through devolving of powers to the states. A vast reservoir of People's Power has not yet been tested in the real sense. We have not been able to involve the people in Governance as functionaries and facilitators.

- People's Participation: Our developmental process will be a people's movement - of Jan bhagidari.

We will make them the active drivers of development rather than mere passive recipients.

- People's Engagement: Through Pro-active, Pro-people Good Governance, we will ensure the Government itself directly reaches out to the people, especially the weak and marginalized sections of society.

- We will further evolve the Public Private Partnership (PPP) model into a People-Public-Private Partnership (PPPP) model.

- BJP is committed to strengthen self-Governance at the local level and we will empower Panchayatis.

- Raj Institutions with extensive devolution of the 3 Fs - Functions, Functionaries and Funds.

- Good performers amongst the Panchayats will be rewarded with additional developmental grants.

- Strengthen the institution of the Gram Sabha, respecting their inputs and initiatives for development process.

- We will actively involve people in policy formulation and evaluation through various platforms.

- We will encourage Openness in the Government, involving all stakeholders in the decision-making processes.

Reform the System

Good Governance: Transparent, Effective, Involving and Encouraging

India First

BJP believes in India being one country, one people and one nation. BJP recognizes the importance of diversity in Indian society, and the strength and vibrancy it adds to the nation. The party believes in the principle of unity in diversity.

India constitutes of all its' people, irrespective of caste, creed, religion or sex. It constitutes of all the communities - ethnic, social and cultural groups and also our culture, which is defined by tolerance and co-existence. The hallmark of India is "Unity in Diversity". It constitutes of each and every inch of our land, its natural resources and mental and physical energy we possess. It constitutes of all the institutions made in the past and present.

India First simply means nurturing and protecting all the elements, which India is made of. It does not exclude anyone or anything - it only includes everything and everyone, which India is made of. It is complete India; without exclusion, without exception. It also means that whatever is in the interest of India will be in the interest of all the elements that India is made up of, including its citizens.

The counter to the concept of 'India First' is what is happening today; appeasement of one, at the cost of the other, using Institutions for protecting the interest of a particular party or persons. It is reflected in the thinking that whatever is not in the interest of a party is not in the interest of India. Clearly, Governance on these lines is not in the interest of India.

Simply speaking, 'India First' puts the national interest first while taking any decision or step both by Governments and citizens. Even more simply put, you have to just see the face of India and Indians when you are in doubt. This is what separates 'India First' from the present day politics and Governance of the Congress-led UPA.

For BJP:

- The only philosophy and religion of a Government should be India's First.
- The only epic of a Government should be India's Constitution.
- The only power of a Government should be the power of the people.
- The only prayer of a Government should be the welfare of its people.
- The only way of a Government should be 'Sabka Saath, Sabka Vikas'.

Open Government and Accountable Administration

Administrative reforms will be a priority for the BJP. Hence, we propose to implement them through an appropriate body under the PMO. The objective will be to bring in transparency in Government's decision- making process. Government systems and processes would be relooked to make them citizen friendly, corruption free and accountable. Every effort will be made to meet the development aspirations of the people and make the Government agencies accountable to the citizens. We will set-up an effective Lokpal institution. Corruption at any level will be dealt with firmly and swiftly.

From birth certificate to school admission, from setting up business to paying of taxes, our present systems complicate the lives of our own people. We will reform it and make it easy in terms of access, efficiency and delivery. Following specific action will be initiated:

- Digitization of Government records will be taken up on top priority so that they are easily accessible.
- Performance review, social and environment audit would be mandated for all Government schemes and programmes.

- Open up Government to draw expertise from the industry, academia and society into the services.

- Government will be redefined by elimination of whatever is obsolete in laws, regulations, administrative structures, practices and would be purposive.

- We will generate 'Kartavya Bhavna' among public servants as lives and productivity of people is dependent on the quality and efficiency of public services.

On the whole, hallmarks of our Governance model would be:

- People-centric
- Policy driven
- Time bound delivery
- Minimum Government, Maximum Governance

E-Governance: Easy, Efficient and Effective

BJP believes that IT is a great enabler for empowerment, equity and efficiency. The NDA Government had made IT one of the major thrust areas. With the result, India is the IT capital for the whole world. But back home, the benefits of IT have not percolated down. This will be a high priority area for BJP that IT touches the lives of ordinary men and women. BJP has been known for good Governance and e- Governance will become the backbone for good Governance. BJP aims to nurture a Digital India - making every household and every individual digitally empowered.

Information Technology has made it possible to make information and services reach to the ordinary men and women even in remote areas, easily and effectively. Availability of information is the key to empowerment of the stakeholders. This also reduces the scope for discretion and manipulation.

We will:

- Focus on increasing the penetration and usage of broadband across the country. Deployment of broadband in every village would be a thrust area.

- Leverage technology for e-Governance and engage proactively with the people through social media for participative governance and effective public grievance redressal mechanism.

- Generate IT based jobs in rural and semi-urban areas.

- Make technology enabled products affordable for students.

- Use technology to reduce the burden of books on children. Make all institutions and schools e- enabled in a phased manner. Digital learning and training to be used extensively.

- Pursue a mission mode project under the 'National Rural Internet and Technology Mission' for use of telemedicine and mobile healthcare for rural healthcare delivery; use of IT for agriculture for real time information; Self Help Groups; retail trade and SMEs; and rural entrepreneurs, etc.

- Initiate a National e-Governance Plan to cover every Government office from the centre to the panchayats. The 'E-Gram, Vishwa Gram' scheme in Gujarat to be implemented nationwide.

- Promote e-Bhasha - National Mission for the promotion of IT in Indian Languages.

- Focus to bring SC/ST, OBCs and other weaker sections of the society within the ambit of IT.

Enabled development

- Deploy IT to protect India's priceless cultural and artistic heritage, which includes digitization of all archives and museology.

- Promote 'open source' and 'open standard' software.

- Mandate digitization of all government work to reduce corruption and delays.

- Set up High-speed digital highways to unite the nation.

- Use technology to reduce Transmission and distribution losses.

- Use mobile and e-Banking to ensure financial inclusion.

BJP aims to make every household digitally literate with a goal to make India the Global Knowledge hub, with IT being a major driver and engine of growth.

Institutional Reform - Administrative, Judicial, Police and Electoral

Administrative

Today, people of this country are frustrated with the present system. Our administrative set up should be people-centric, responsive and result-oriented. With this in mind, we are committed to bring the following reforms:

- The administration and its members will be made truly accountable to their tasks as well as the people through rigorous evaluation process.

- Good performance will be rewarded; non-performers will be given opportunities and training support to improve.

- Rationalization and convergence among the Ministries, departments and other arms of the Government will be ensured to focus on delivery.

- Open up government to draw expertise from the industry, academia and society.

- Services of youth in particular will be tapped to contribute in governance with Fellowship and Internship programmes launched at various levels.

Judicial

BJP is committed to ensure Justice for all - justice which is prompt and accessible. Understanding that Justice Delayed is Justice Denied, we will adopt a multi-pronged approach to address the high pendency of cases in our judicial system.

We will:

- Accord high priority to judicial reforms to address the issue of appointment of judges, filling the vacancies, opening new courts, setting up a mechanism for speedy clearance of the backlog of cases at various levels in the judiciary.

- Initiate a mission mode project for filling the vacancies in the judiciary and for doubling the number of courts and judges in the subordinate judiciary.

- Set up a National Judicial Commission for the appointment of judges in higher judiciary.

- Create a fund for modernization of courts to improve the operational efficiency of courts.

- Set up a separate class of courts for cases involving specified commercial laws which fast track the litigation process.

- Reform the criminal justice system to make dispensation of justice simpler, quicker and more effective and after examining the recommendations of the earlier reports on this subject.

- Initiate the computerization and networking of courts all over the country.

- Extend fast track courts at every stage of the judiciary.

- Expand alternative dispute redressal mechanisms through Lok Adalat and Tribunals.

- Implement the National Litigation Policy in letter and spirit to reduce average pendency time of cases.

- Review and reduce significantly the number of cases, in which the Government is a litigant in the next five years.

- Periodically review and refine/ scrap outdated laws.

- Create courts specially equipped to deal with IPR cases.

- Give special emphasis to the development of Alternate Dispute Resolution mechanisms - like

- Lok Adalat, Arbitration and Conciliation centres.

- Set up a comprehensive National e-Library, empowering Lawyers.

- Aim to enhance the number of women in the Bar as well as Bench, reducing the gender gap in judiciary.

- Evolve a national network of specialized universities having expertise in complementary domains.

- Like Forensics, Arbitration, IPR, International Law, etc.

- Develop India into a Global Hub for Arbitration and Legal Process Outsourcing.

- We will simultaneously reform the legal system to make it more accessible to the common man. We will:

- Undertake a comprehensive review of the legal system to simplify complex legislations - converge overlapping legislation, as well as remove contradictory and redundant laws.

- Establish an institutional mechanism to periodically review and give suggestions for refining our laws.

- Simplify legal procedure and language.

- Make legal information open and freely accessible.

- Run legal awareness programmes and introduce in school curriculum - making the common man aware of his rights and duties.

Police

Our police forces are entrusted with the crucial responsibility of maintaining law and public order, which forms one of the central pillars of our democracy. We will work with the states to empower them with the authority, independence and resources necessary to deliver:

- Roll out a comprehensive strategy for bringing the Indian Police at par with international standards.
- Facilitate training and capacity building of Police forces.
- Modernize the police force, equipping them with the latest technology.
- Initiate the networking of police stations across the country for intelligence sharing and crime control.
- Strengthen Investigations, making them Swift, Transparent, Fair, Clear and Decisive - acting as an inescapable deterrent to wrong- doers and a protective shield to the innocent.
- Develop specialized expertise in investigation; through continuous training, especially in evolving competencies.
- Overhaul our intelligence set up, with special focus on coordination and integration of human and technological intel - comprehensively gearing it towards collecting real time, specific and actionable inputs.
- Modernize our Prison system with technology and infrastructure; to strengthen the security as well human rights and correctional dimensions.
- Work towards evolving common national standards and protocols.
- Train and technologically enable the police to track, pursue, as well as prevent Cyber Crime.
- Bring Coastal States together on a common platform to discuss issues of Marine Policing.
- Reinterpret the age-old concept of community policing in modern times; evolving ways for the police to reach out to the people, building bonds of trust and friendship - including spreading out into areas of public safety and public wellness.
- Give special emphasis for improving the working conditions and welfare of police personnel.

Electoral

BJP is committed to initiate electoral reforms to eliminate criminals. The BJP will seek, through consultation with other parties, to evolve a method of holding Assembly and Lok Sabha elections simultaneously. Apart from reducing election expenses for both political parties and Government, this will ensure certain stability for State Governments. We will also look at revising expenditure limits realistically.

Widen the Platform

Certain segments of India have been historically disadvantaged. Due to a lopsided development approach and skewed allocation of resources, they continue to lag behind the rest of the country in socio- economic indicators in spite of having abundant natural resources and talent. Consequently, our demographic dividend is not being fully actualized. It is the duty of the government to enable every Indian to realize his or her full potential, ensuring equitable growth and development. We are committed towards this end, and will ensure the same by:

- Empowering each and every Indian through health and education.
- Increasing Opportunities by making Job creation central to our economic model.
- Ensuring a basic level of Infrastructure to all - Home, Electricity, Water, Toilets and Access.

Poor and Marginalized - Bridge the Gap

Our Government will be a government of the poor, marginalized and left behind. Every Indian has a right over everything that India has. From this, he or she is free to weave his or her own dreams. The India of tomorrow will have 125 crore such dreams, and will be built on the same. We will not only empower our citizens with the ability to dream; we will enable them with the capability to actualize their dreams.

The real test of the success of a development process lies in the happiness of the common man. The fruits of growth and development must reach the weakest, most deprived and remotest of people. With firm belief in the concept of Antyodaya - uplifting the poorest of the poor - Extreme Poverty and malnutrition will be treated as a National priority, and will be addressed on Mission Mode.

We will:

- Strengthen Delivery of poverty alleviation programs through convergence, transparency and efficiency.
- Identify 100 most backward districts of the country to bring them at par with other districts through prioritized and integrated development.
- Strengthen the natural resource base of the people to tide over natural calamities.
- Aim to gainfully employ rural poor in agriculture and allied activities.
- Enable the urban poor to develop skills so that they take an advantage of the emerging opportunities.
- Facilitate partnership across all levels of government, civil society, academic and financial institutions in this national mission of poverty alleviation.

Food Security

BJP has always held that 'universal food security' is an integral to national security. BJP will take steps to ensure that the benefits of the scheme should reach the common man and that the right to food does not remain an act on paper or a political rhetoric. BJP will review all the laws and schemes, in consultation with the states, to ensure a corruption-free efficient implementation of food security, which would be a priority.

BJP will:

- Review the successful PDS models and incorporate the best practices to revise the existing PDS for benefitting the common man.
- Address the issue of under-nutrition and malnutrition.
- Encourage the production of cereals, pulses and oils.
- Radically transform the Food Corporation of India (FCI).

- Ensure contingency stocks for any exigencies arising due to natural calamities or external factors.

- Seek the participation of voluntary organizations in running community kitchens.

SCs, STs, OBCs and Other Weaker Sections - Social Justice and Empowerment

The BJP is committed to bridge the gap, following the principles of Samajik Nyay (social justice) and Samajik Samrasata (social harmony). This social justice must be further complemented with economic justice and political empowerment. Instead of pursuing identity politics and tokenisms, we will focus on empowering the deprived sections of society. Steps will be taken to create an enabling ecosystem of equal opportunity - for education, health and livelihood. We will accord highest priority to ensuring their security, especially the prevention of atrocities against SCs & STs.

We believe that accelerated social justice and integrated development is the key to the progress of our country and success of our democracy. The BJP is committed to bridge the divide following the principle of social justice (Samajik Nyay) and social harmony (Samajik Samrasata). Instead of pursuing identity politics and tokenisms, which have not led to any tangible results for the SC, ST, OBCs and other weaker sections of our society, the BJP will focus on tangible development and empowerment.

- A high priority for SC, ST, OBCs and other weaker sections would be to create an ecosystem for education and entrepreneurship.

- BJP is committed to the eradication of untouchability at all levels.

- BJP is committed to eliminate manual scavenging.

- BJP will look at more effective ways to pull these people out of the poverty line.

- BJP will ensure that the funds allocated for schemes and programmes for SC, ST, OBCs and other weaker sections are utilized properly.

- A mission mode project would be made for housing, education, health and skills development.

- Special focus would be on the children, especially the girl child, with regards to health, education and skills development.

Tribal development will be one of the focus areas. BJP believes that half-hearted, incremental and piecemeal attempts for the development of tribals have not helped. So the BJP commits to make a comprehensive, all-encompassing long-term strategy to empower tribals and ensure their welfare. The goal would be to ensure tribal development while preserving the unique identities of this community. The Governments of Gujarat, Madhya Pradesh and Chhattisgarh have successfully implemented the tribal welfare and development schemes and their model would be used for tribal welfare and development.

BJP will initiate a 'Van Bandhu Kalyan Yojana' at the national level to be overseen by a 'Tribal Development Authority'. This scheme will focus on:

- Setting up the entire education network for tribals.
- Upgrading housing, water and health facilities.
- Electrification of tribal hamlets and provision of all - weather roads.
- Initiating new economic activities.
- Promoting the products associated with the tribal culture by setting tribal haats in tourist towns and other centres.
- Ensure that the tribal land is not alienated.
- Facilitating access to minor forest produce and creating a network of rural haats (markets).
- Establishing the National Centre for Tribal Research and Culture to preserve the tribal culture and languages.
- Enhancing the funds for tribal welfare and development.

Minorities - Equal Opportunity

BJP believes that in India's 'Unity in Diversity' lies India's biggest strength. We cherish the depth and vibrancy that the diversity in Indian society adds to the nation. BJP is thus committed to the preservation of the rich culture and heritage of India's minority communities; alongside their social and economic empowerment.

It is unfortunate that even after several decades of independence, a large section of the minority, especially Muslim community, continues to be stymied in poverty. Modern India must be a nation of equal opportunity. BJP is committed to ensure that all communities are equal partners in India's progress, as we believe India cannot progress if any segment of Indians is left behind.

We will:

- Ensure that the young and the girl child in particular get education and jobs without discrimination.
- Strengthen and modernize minority educational systems and institutions; dovetailing them with modern requirements. National Madrasa modernization programme would be initiated.
- Empower with vibrancy in Livelihood and Entrepreneurial opportunities.
- Augment their traditional artisanship and entrepreneurial skill, which are a backbone of our cottage and small-scale industry - strengthening these sectors through better market linkages, branding and access to credit.
- Empower Waqf Boards in consultation with religious leaders; taking steps to remove encroachments from and unauthorized occupation of Waqf properties.
- Curate their rich heritage and culture - maintenance and restoration of heritage sites; digitization of archives; preservation and promotion of Urdu.
- Ensure a peaceful and secure environment, where there is no place for either the perpetrators or exploiters of fear.
- Facilitate the setting up of a permanent Inter-faith Consultative mechanism to promote harmony and trust under the auspices of religious leaders.

Neo-Middle Class - Meet their Aspirations

India has a large middle class with immense understanding, talent and purchasing power. In addition, a whole new class has emerged. Those who have risen from the category of poor and are yet to stabilize in the middle class, the 'neo middle class'. This class needs proactive handholding. Having moved out of poverty, their aspirations have increased. They want amenities and services of a certain standard. They thus now feel that Government facilities and services are not up to the mark, and hence resort to the private sector for things like education, health and transport. This is obviously costly, putting the neo middle class into a daily dilemma. As more and more people move into this category, their expectations for better public services have to be met. We have to strengthen the Public Sector for providing efficient services to our citizens. In particular, attention will be paid on government providing:

- Educational scholarships and educational facilities.
- Medical insurance and quality healthcare services.
- Middle-income housing.
- Efficient public transport systems.

Rural Areas - High Priority

Two-thirds of our people live in villages. Lack of amenities to live and opportunities to work, however, are restricting our rural life. Both these factors are the result of prolonged neglect. A full-fledged programme for 'Rural Rejuvenation' will be made and implemented which will comprise of integrated strategies for personal, economic and social well-being of the villagers. Through the idea of Rurban, we will bring urban amenities to our rural areas, while retaining the soul of the village.

Agriculture, rural development and poverty alleviation go hand in hand. Major thrust area for rural development would be to improve village level infrastructure in terms of roads, potable water, education, health, supply chain, electricity, broadband, job creation, security in rural areas and linkage to markets.

Urban Areas - High Growth Centres

More than one-third of our population is already living in our cities and towns. Soon, the urban areas will cover half our people. Moreover, our cities should no longer remain a reflection of poverty and bottlenecks. Rather they should become symbols of efficiency, speed and scale.

- We will look at urbanisation as an Opportunity rather than a Threat.

- Major steps will be undertaken in Transport and Housing for 'Urban Upliftment' in India.

- We will initiate building 100 new cities; enabled with the latest in technology and infrastructure - adhering to concepts like sustainability, walk to work etc, and focused on specialized domains.

- The approach to urban development will be based on integrated habitat development - building on concepts like Twin cities and Satellite towns.

- Upgrade existing urban centres, transitioning focus from basic infrastructure to public utility services like Waste and Water Management - for a clean and healthy city life.

- Cleanliness and Sanitation will be given priority - efficient Waste and Water management systems will be set up. Model towns will be identified for rolling out integrated waste management infrastructure.

- Wi-Fi facilities will be made available in public places and commercial centres.

- Urban poverty alleviation scheme would be a key thrust area.

- Use technology for scientific, strategic and long term town planning - including GIS based mapping.

- Build quality integrated Public Transport systems, discouraging usage of private vehicles.

Leap Forward

We have to give the taste of a developed country to this very generation. We have to take a quantitative and qualitative leap. The time of knee jerk reactions and incremental changes has gone. What we need is a quantum jump and a total change. We also believe that development has to be holistic, uniform and all pervasive. Further, we have to make the people active partners in whatever is happening and empower them to take advantage of the development process. We will make an effort that government withdraws from those services which could be done by others and devote that extra time, money and energy for social sectors, particularly for development of the weaker sections. And a common thread will run across all our ideas and initiatives. This common thread is the wire and wave of Technology - maximum application of technology for making governance easy, economical and effective.

Social Security - A Caring Government, Passionate Society

India has always been a caring society. It is in our culture to help the aged, the weak and the helpless. We have to retain this. We have to educate our younger generations about this. The social security schemes of the Governments have to be made more meaningful. Our aspirations get frustrated when we encounter a weak social infrastructure. We need it on a daily basis.

Children - the Future of the Nation

"There can be no keener revelation of a society's soul than the way in which it treats its children" - Nelson Mandela

Indicators related to children welfare are an indicator of the progress of the nation, be it health, education or safety of children. Under the UPA rule, the same has not been given its due weightage. BJP is committed to address the issues related to children, like malnutrition and under-nutrition, problem of child labour, child-trafficking and missing children, sexual abuse, school dropouts and the increasing crime rate among juveniles. BJP will take the following steps to ensure survival, development, participation and protection of children:

- Lay special emphasis on vulnerable children and especially those belonging to the vulnerable communities like SCs, STs, OBCs, migrants, slum dwellers, street dwellers and those with disabilities.
- Ensure effective implementation of the Right to Education, Right to Food Security Act.
- Review, amend and strengthen the Child and Adolescent Labour (Prohibition and Regulation) Act, 2012 and Integrated Child Protection Scheme (ICPS).
- Focused efforts will be made to address issue of anaemia.
- Reduce the burden of books on children without compromising on the quality of education.
- Endeavour to inculcate values amongst children.

Senior Citizens

BJP is committed to the welfare of senior citizens, especially their security and health care. We will take measures to deal with the issues related to the senior citizens in a focused manner.

BJP will:

- Provide financial support, exploring ideas like additional tax benefits and higher interest rates.

- Invest in setting up and improving old-age homes.

- Harness their experience in the National Interest. Devise schemes and programs to engage the senior citizens as volunteers / part time workers in various development programmes of the government, in urban and rural areas. This will not only help in utilizing their time, but also it would be an effective utilization of their experience and may add an additional source of income for them.

Specially Abled

About 70 million people are suffering from disability and BJP considers it a serious neglect. The welfare and rehabilitation of disabled people is integral to our vision of a caring society and that of a responsive government. The BJP commits to:

- Enact the 'Rights of the Persons with Disabilities bill' (RPWD).

- Use technology to deliver low cost quality education to specially-abled students 'in-home' - through E-learning.

- Identify each and every special needs person across the country - establishing a web based disability registration system to issue universal ID for all applicable government benefits (healthcare, transportation, jobs, education etc).

- Ensure disabled friendly access to public facilities, public buildings and transport.

- Ensure maximum economic independence of the disabled by creating more income generation models for them.

- Support and aid voluntary organizations working for the care of the disabled.

- Provide a higher tax relief for the family member taking care of the disabled.

Youth - Making India Unstoppable

'Young men, my hope is in you. Will you respond to the call of your nation? Each one of you has a glorious future if you dare believe me. Have a tremendous faith in yourselves, like the faith I had when I was a child and which I am working out now. Have that faith, each one of you, in yourself-that eternal power is lodged in every soul-and you will revive the whole of the country.' - Swami Vivekananda

BJP considers youth as the most productive asset of the nation who have played a key role in taking the country to a near double digit growth. All sectors dominated by youth are doing exceptionally well. India is the oldest civilization but the youngest country and this necessitates that the policies must be based on the judicious mix of experience of energy, and be 'Youth inclusive', so that youth are an integral part of the development process. We commit to review and revise policies to seek participation of youth in decision-making and nation building process and actively get the youth to participate in decision-making bodies.

- We will initiate the 'Young Leaders programme' in all sectors, to recognize, reward and involve these exceptionally talented youth to serve as role models and mentors for others.
- Set up the National Youth Advisory Council.
- BJP will initiate nation-wide 'district level incubation and accelerator programme' for encouraging innovation and entrepreneurship.
- Procedure to avail Student's loans will be simplified and loans made affordable.
- Set up neighbourhood Children's/ Youth Parliament across India that leads to vibrant student committees.
- Will launch a programme, 'Youth for Development'.

Promotion of Sports

BJP recognizes the importance of sports in society and for all age groups. Sports have a direct relation to fitness, good health and productivity. India has not fared well in sports, and needs to invest for promotion of sports in an organized manner.

- BJP will promote all sports - traditional and modern.
- More funds will be allocated to sports, and we will encourage the State Governments to fully discharge their responsibility in the promotion of sports.
- Steps would be taken to inculcate a culture of sports at the school level by arranging sports facilities and training needs for promoting a healthy lifestyle and making sports as a compulsory part of the school curriculum.
- Launch a 'National Sports Talent Search System', so that extraordinary sporting talent is identified at a very young age. Such promising boys and girls will be selected for special training. The existing rural sports programme and National Women Sports Festival will be broadened to reach every village and to identify talent for nurturing and excellence development.
- Attractive career path needs to be planned for sportspersons providing security of career through jobs in government, PSUs and private sector.
- Establish sports academies across the country.
- Special scheme would be devised for sportspersons to ensure social security.
- Encourage business houses to patronize sports and sportspersons.
- Mandate all new housing colonies to include sports facilities.

Women - The Nation Builders

BJP recognizes the important role of women in development of the society and growth of the nation, and remains committed to give a high priority to Women's Empowerment and welfare. BJP ruled states have demonstrated this through various schemes. BJP also recognizes the need for women's security as a precondition to women's empowerment and will undertake the following for women welfare:

- Women's welfare and development will be accorded a high priority at all levels within the government, and BJP is committed to 33% reservation in parliamentary and state assemblies through a constitutional amendment.

- Launch a national campaign for saving the girl child and educating her - 'Beti Bachao - Beti Padhao'.

- Structure a comprehensive scheme, incorporating best practices from past successes like Balika Samruddhi, Ladli Laxmi and Chiranjeevi Yojana to support encourage positive attitude amongst families towards the girl child.

- Program for women healthcare in a mission mode, especially focusing on domains of Nutrition and Pregnancy - with emphasis on Rural, SCs, STs and OBCs.

- We will enable women with training and skills - setting up dedicated Women ITIs, Women wings in other ITIs.

- Strict implementation of laws related to women, particularly those related to rape.

- Fund for relief and rehabilitation of rape victims' lies unused at the Centre as the Government has not worked out the modalities of dispensation. BJP will clear this on priority.

- Government will create an Acid Attack victims welfare fund to take care of the medical costs related to treatment and cosmetic reconstructive surgeries of such victims.

- Make police stations women friendly and increase the number of women in police at different levels.

- Introduce self-defence as a part of the school curriculum.

- Using information technology for women's safety.

- Set up an All Women Mobile Bank to cater to women.

- Special skills training and business incubator park for women.

- Setting up special business facilitation centre for women.

- Expand and improve upon the network of women / working women hostels.

- Set up a dedicated W-SME (Women Small and Medium Enterprises) cluster in every district.

- Review the working conditions and enhance the remuneration of Anganwadi worker's.

- Remove any remaining gender disparities in property rights, marital rights and cohabitation rights.

- Special adult literacy initiative would be started for women with focus on SCs, STs, OBCs, and slum residents.

- Will ensure that the loans to Women Self Help Groups would be available at low interest rates.

- Special programs aimed at girls below poverty line, tribals and indigent women.

- Appropriate measures would be taken to check female foeticide, dowry, child marriage, trafficking, sexual harassment, rape and family violence.

- We will transform the quality of life of women in Rural India by providing electricity, tapped water, cleaner fuel and toilets in every home.

Education - Enrol and Excel

BJP believes that education is the most powerful tool for the advancement of the nation and the most potent weapon to fight poverty. Education in India needs to be revitalized and reorganized to make future generations proud of their culture, heritage and history and also for creating confidence in the vitality of India. Every effort shall be made to ensure 'equality of opportunity in access and success' to all learners; creating a harmonious, and cohesive egalitarian society that practices democratic values. This would be possible only when Education accords due emphasis on national integration, social cohesion, religious amity, national identity and patriotism. It must also be analysed how far education has contributed to moral, ethical and humanistic values in the individuals and the society.

Education must create minds free from superstitions, hatred and violence and become an important vehicle to cement national unity, social cohesion and religious amity. Our endeavour should be to inculcate moral, ethical and humanistic values in the individuals and the society.

India has to become a knowledge society and has to reverberate with educated skilled manpower of high standards required to meet the challenges of 21st century. This requires a bold and visionary leadership to introduce appropriate policy and structural changes.

Highest priority would be given to address the acute shortage of teachers and researchers, quality of education and research, and also the employability factor associated with most of the courses. Education should not only lead to employability but also job creation and entrepreneurship by introducing a national multi-skills orientation program.

We intend to review and revise education system; the salary structures associated with the teaching staff and most importantly, address the shortfall of faculty and related issues in the country. The system shall be made people-friendly and the credibility of the system shall be restored.

Investment in education yields the best dividend. Public spending on education would be raised to 6% of the GDP, and involving the private sector would further enhance this.

Under the scheme of 'Quality education for all', BJP would take the following steps;

School Education

- NDA's flagship program 'Sarva Shiksha Abhiyan': Mechanism would be set up for its performance audit and to have real time information about its performance. Programme shall be strengthened and expanded with a goal to remove illiteracy.
- Universalization of secondary school education and skills development through functional school shall be seriously pursued with particular focus on rural, tribal and difficult areas.
- The content and process of school education shall be thoroughly reviewed to make it dynamic, stress-free, attractive and responsive to the emerging national needs.
- Girls shall be provided all possible help to continue and complete school education.
- The digital divide shall not be allowed to create further divisions in the learning situations of children.
- Special pedagogy would be developed for differently-abled students.
- On priority, a national modernization programme for madrasa's would be started.
- Mid-day meal scheme would be revitalized in terms of management and delivery.
- We will explore ways to reduce the daily burden of carrying books to school for children, which would also entail use of technology for education as a mission mode project.
- Establish a national E-Library to empower school teachers and students.

- Initiate a multi-country student exchange programme for broadening the horizon of school going children.

- Creative talents of students will be recognized and encouraged.

Higher and Professional Education

The basic objective of higher and professional education is not only rapid advancement of the affluent sector of the society but also to improve the lot of the last man in the line.

The content should be designed to prepare the students to understand the current challenges and equip themselves to be able to readily adjust in a fast changing global scenario. Policy interventions would include:

- Enhancing the pivotal role of the teachers by reworking the work culture of teacher training institutions with a goal to prepare committed and performing teachers.

- Optimum utilization of physical and manpower resources.

- A mechanism for close interaction between industry (including SME), academia and community would be instituted.

- Needs assessment exercise will be done for identifying the future needs across sectors, and the same would be used for developing appropriate courses for higher education, to ensure that the country has adequate manpower for every sector, both established and emerging, in the economy.

- Will provide autonomy with steps to ensure accountability for institutions of higher learning.

- Will raise the standard of education and research, so that Indian universities become at par with the top global universities and find their place in the global league.

- The credibility of the regulatory bodies shall be restored. The procedures to make appointments to senior positions shall be made transparent and merit and ability shall be the sole criterion.

- UGC will be restructured and it will be transformed into a Higher Education Commission rather than just being a grant distribution agency.

- We will revisit the Apprenticeship Act to facilitate our youth to Earn while they Learn.

Vocational Training

- Would set up Massive Open Online Courses (MOOC) and virtual classrooms to make it convenient for working class people and housewives to further develop their knowledge and qualifications.

- Correspondence courses will be started in new domains for self-employment; family run businesses, entrepreneurship and innovation, and these courses would be provided for free to women. The goal would be to prepare the youth for jobs being created by the emerging sectors, foster a spirit of innovation and entrepreneurship, leading to more incomes and job creation.

BJP will set up a National Commission on Education to report in two years on the state of education and the reforms needed. Based on the report, BJP will implement a National Education Policy to meet the changing dynamics of the population's requirement with regards to quality education, innovation and research, aiming to make India a knowledge superpower by equipping its students with the necessary skills and knowledge and to eliminate the shortage of manpower in science, technology, academics and industry.

Skills - Focusing on Productivity and Employability

Skilful hands, bright minds, discipline and perseverance makes Indian talent an asset worldwide. We have to live up to this potential, preparing the World's Largest Workforce. We have to make our youth productively employed and gainfully engaged. We also have to develop India as a Knowledge Powerhouse. We have to train and nurture our human resource. We have to use it for leap-frogging our Nation into the future. Unfortunately, the initiatives taken by Congress for this have fallen woefully short, being almost non-starters.

- We will take up skill development on a mission mode, at an unprecedented scale.

- Skill Mapping - to help scientifically plan our national human resource development that India would need (like engineers, architects, doctors, nurses, lawyers, accountants, plumbers, carpenters, welders, etc.).

- Launch a 'National Multi-skill Mission'

- We will run short-term courses, in the evenings, focusing on employable skills.

- We will also set up Centres of Excellence in various sectors in partnership with the Industry.

- To ensure industry responsive manpower, we will bring together industry, universities and government.

- We will promote vocational training on a massive scale. Rigid segregation of formal education and skill development will be broken; a mechanism will be established to give vocational qualifications of Academic Equivalence.

- We will also create institutional mechanisms to refresh and upgrade abilities through continuing education - to make them employable.

- We will focus on need based skill development and employability; making our youth employable even in the most sophisticated jobs.

We will:

- Put emphasis on imparting soft skills to enhance employability including a national program on foreign languages.

- Launch a national programme for digital empowerment through computer literacy of the people, especially the youth.

- We will assess the talent and capacity of our youth from an early age; so they can be groomed accordingly.

- We will push for greater practical and research training encouraging real world experience through internships and apprenticeships.

Health Services - Increase the Access, Improve the Quality, and Lower the Cost

India needs a holistic care system that is universally accessible, affordable and effective and drastically reduces the out of pocket spending on health. NRHM has failed to meet the objectives and will be radically reformed. BJP accords high priority to health sector, which is crucial for securing the economy.

The overarching goal of healthcare would be to provide, 'Health Assurance to all Indians and to reduce the out of pocket spending on health care', with the help of state governments.

The current situation calls for radical reforms in the healthcare system with regards to national healthcare programs and delivery, medical education and training and financing of healthcare. Our government would focus on the following reforms in healthcare:

- The last healthcare policy dates back to 2002. India now needs a comprehensive healthcare policy to address the complex healthcare challenges, keeping in view the developments in the healthcare sector and the changing demographics. BJP will initiate the New Health Policy.

- Initiate the 'National Health Assurance Mission', with a clear mandate to provide universal healthcare that is not only accessible and affordable, but also effective, and reduces the OOP spending for the common man.

- Education and Training - Will review the role of various professional regulatory bodies in healthcare and consider setting up an overarching lean body for healthcare. High priority will be given to address the shortfall of healthcare professionals.

- Modernize Government hospitals, upgrading infrastructure and latest technologies.

- Reorganize Ministry of Health and Family Welfare in order to converge various departments dealing in healthcare, food and nutrition and pharmaceuticals, for effective delivery of healthcare services.

- Increase the number of medical and para-medical colleges to make India self-sufficient in human resources and set up an AIIMS like institute in every state.

- Yoga and Ayurveda are the gifts of ancient Indian civilization to humanity and we will increase the public investment to promote Yoga and AYUSH. We will start integrated courses for Indian System of Medicine (ISM) and modern science and Ayurgenomics. We will set up institutions and launch a vigorous program to standardize and validate the Ayurvedic medicine.

- Move to pre-emptive care model where the focus and thrust will be on child health and prevention.

- School health program would be a major focus area and health and hygiene will be made a part of the school curriculum.

- Focus on Rural Health care delivery.

- Senior Citizens healthcare would be a special focus area.

- Give high priority to chronic diseases, and will invest in research and development of solutions for chronic diseases like obesity, diabetes, cancer, CVD etc.

- Occupational health programs will be pursued aggressively.

- Utilize the ubiquitous platform of mobile phones for healthcare delivery and set up the 'National eHealth Authority' to leverage telemedicine and mobile healthcare for expanding reach and coverage and to define the standards and legal framework for technology driven care.

- Universalization of emergency medical services-108.

- Re-orientation of herbal plants board to encourage farming of herbal plants.

- Population stabilization would be a major thrust area and would be pursued as a mission mode program.

- Programme for Women Healthcare with emphasis on rural, SC, ST and OBC in a mission mode.

- Mission mode project to eradicate malnutrition.

- Launch National Mosquito Control mission.

Poor Hygiene and Sanitation have a far reaching, cascading impact. We will ensure a 'Swachh Bharat' by Gandhiji's 150th birth anniversary in 2019, taking it up in mission mode by converging resources and building around Jan bhagidari:

- Create an open defecation free India by awareness campaign and enabling people to build toilets in their home as well as in schools and public places.

- Set up modern, scientific sewage and waste management systems.

- We will introduce Sanitation Ratings measuring and ranking our cities and towns on 'sanitation' and rewarding the best performers.

- Make potable drinking water available to all thus reducing water-borne diseases, which will automatically translate into Diarrhoea-free India.

Economic Revival

When the NDA Government completed its tenure the baton was handed over to the incoming UPA Government with GDP growth nearing double digit in 2004. Inflation was under control. Fiscal Deficit and Current Account Deficit were kept within limit and the overall Economy was showing robust fundamentals. In contrast, now at the end of Congress-led UPA regime, the GDP growth has plummeted to very low of 4.8%, the inflation and price rise beyond control, the fiscal deficit and current account deficit in the alarm zone, and the manufacturing sector facing a recession. The Congress-led UPA has indulged in massive scams during its last five years. In recent years, the Indian Rupee has seen a free fall like never before.

This is basically the result of policy and decision paralysis of the UPA Government. Decisions are simply not taken. And if they are taken, they turn into scandals. All this has destroyed the reputation of our economy. To reverse this process, the first thing, which is required, is to restore confidence in the integrity of the decision-making and sanctity of our decisions.

We will bring back credibility and trust in government, re-sowing confidence in the India story domestically as well as internationally. Through consistent, long-term policies, we will not just spur the process of economic growth, but also ensure that it is stable as well as balanced.

We will:

- Find out solutions, which are effective in the short run and lasting in the long run.
- Strictly implement Fiscal discipline, without compromising on funds availability for development work and asset creation.
- Allocate resources efficiently and effectively to re-energize the engines of growth.
- Re-visit the policy framework for investments both foreign and domestic to make them more conducive.
- Undertake Banking reforms to enhance ease and access, as well as accountability.
- We will encourage Savings as an important driver of investment and growth.

NPAs

NPAs have increased sharply over the past few years and the trend continues. BJP will take necessary steps to reduce NPAs in Banking sector. Also, BJP will set up a strong regulatory framework for the non-banking financial companies to protect the investors.

Taxation

UPA Government has unleashed 'Tax terrorism' and 'uncertainty', which not only creates anxiety amongst the business class and negatively impacts the investment climate, but also dents the image of the country. BJP realizes the importance of having a Tax Policy Roadmap, so that people are aware of the future and plan accordingly.

We will:

- Provide a non-adversarial and conducive tax environment
- Rationalize and simplify the tax regime
- Overhaul the dispute resolution mechanisms
- Bring on board all State governments in adopting GST, addressing all their concerns.
- Provide tax incentives for investments in research and development, geared towards indigenization of technology and innovation.

Foreign Direct Investment

Barring the multi-brand retail sector, FDI will be allowed in sectors wherever needed for job and asset creation, infrastructure and acquisition of niche technology and specialized expertise. BJP is committed to protect the interest of small and medium retailers, SMEs and those employed by them. The FIPBs (Foreign Investment Promotion Board) functioning shall be made more efficient and investor- friendly.

Agriculture - Productive, Scientific and Rewarding

Agriculture is the engine of India's economic growth and the largest employer, and BJP commits highest priority to agricultural growth, increase in farmer's income and rural development.

BJP will:

- Increase public investment in agriculture and rural development.

- Take steps to enhance the profitability in agriculture by ensuring a minimum of 50% profits over the cost of production, cheaper agriculture inputs and credit; introducing latest technologies for farming and high yielding seeds and linking MGNREGA to agriculture.

- Put in place welfare measures for farmers above 60 years in age, small and marginal farmers and farm labours.

- Introduce and promote low water consuming irrigation techniques and optimum utilization of water resources.

- Introduce soil assessment based crop planning and setting up mobile soil testing labs.

- Re-orient pest management and control programmes.

- Implement and incentivize the setting up of the food processing industry that has remained just a plain talk till now. This will lead to better income for farmers and create jobs. We aim to set up 'agro food processing clusters', with high value, export-quality and vacuum packed food processing facilities, etc.

- Focus on the quality, productivity and trade of spices.

- Set up the 'Organic Farming and Fertilizer Corporation of India', to promote organic farming and fertilizers, and provide incentives and support for marketing organic produce.

- Introduce rotation farming for herbal products, based on geographical mapping, to enhance the income of farmers.

- Implement a farm insurance scheme to take care of crop loss due to unforeseen natural calamities.

- Strengthen and expand rural credit facilities.

- Promote horticulture, floriculture, pisciculture, bee-keeping and poultry for generating jobs and income for rural India.

- Promote fish farming and aqua culture. Measures would be taken for the welfare of fisherman.

- Create Cluster based storage systems (e.g. Rice cluster, Wheat Cluster, Veg - Fruit cluster, Spices cluster).

- Introduce the concept of consumer friendly farmers' market to reduce wastages and increase incomes and risk coverage.

- Reform the APMC act.

- Work with the states to set up seed culture labs in each district and regional agriculture innovation labs to conserve agro-biodiversity and to identify and preserve rare indigenous varieties.

- Explore setting up of regional Kisan TV channels.

- Give high priority to poverty alleviation in rural areas.

Genetically Modified (GM) foods will not be allowed without full scientific evaluation on its long-term effects on soil, production and biological impact on consumers.

Land acquisition is a contentious issue due to the opacity of the land acquisition process. BJP will adopt a 'National Land Use Policy', which will look at the scientific acquisition of non-cultivable land and its development; protect the interest of farmers and keep in mind the food production goals and economic goals of the country. Its implementation would be monitored by the National Land Use Authority, which will work with the State Land Use Authorities to regulate and facilitate land management. The power and functions of the National Land Use Authority would be similar to those of other regulatory bodies.

Industry - Modern, Competitive and Caring

We should no longer remain a market for the global industry. Rather, we should become a Global Manufacturing Hub. We have to encourage our industry to innovate and collaborate internationally. We have to encourage industry to produce efficiently and cost-effectively.

Economic freedom implies that Government will not get in the way of the freedom of individuals to start and operate legitimate businesses. Increased economic freedom will break open the economic space to new entrants, especially in the form of small and medium-enterprises, creating jobs and prosperity.

Particularly:

- We will ensure that a conducive, enabling environment is created making 'doing business' in India easy.

- We will focus on cutting the red tape, simplifying the procedures and removing the bottle- necks.

- We will ensure logistics infrastructure, including stable power.

- Our attempt will be to move towards a single-window system of clearances both at the centre and also at the State level through a Hub-spoke model.

- We will put in place a mechanism that will ensure that the Central and state governments work in close coordination and synergy while giving clearances to mega projects.

- Decision-making on environment clearances will be made transparent as well as time-bound.

- We will set up World class Investment and Industrial regions as Global Hubs of Manufacturing.

- We will set up a task force to review and revive our MSME sector (Micro and Small Medium scale Enterprises); enabling it with better access to formal credit and technology for modernization.

- Frame the environment laws in a manner that provides no scope for confusion and will lead to speedy clearance of proposals without delay.

Manufacturing

A strong manufacturing sector will not only bridge the demand-supply gap leading to price stabilization, but also create millions of jobs and increase incomes for the working class. Above all, it will increase the revenue for government and lead to import substitution to bring down the import bill. We will make India a hub for cost-competitive labour-intensive mass manufacturing.

To give boost to manufacturing, BJP will:

- Accord high priority to the growth of manufacturing, so that we can create enough jobs in the country. This sector must grow fast to ensure employment and asset creation.

- Take steps for Interest rate rationalization and have a clear tax policy to remove uncertainty and create investor confidence.

- Take all steps; like removing red-tapism involved in approvals, to make it easy to do business, invest in logistics infrastructure, ensure power supply and undertake labour reforms, besides other steps to create a conducive environment for investors.

- Increase the public spending on R&D and Incentivize R&D investments by the industry to increase the competitiveness of the manufacturing sector.

- We will facilitate setting up of software and hardware manufacturing units.

- Encourage Indian companies to go global and we will support Indian companies in this endeavour.

We believe that Indian entrepreneurs have the capability to take on global markets.

- Set up trade facilitation to ensure easier customs clearances and visas for business travel.

- Initiate a Government - Industry Dialogue, a channel for regular interface with the industry.

MSMEs (Micro, small and medium enterprises)

BJP considers that the role of SME sector is crucial for the economic development of our country. The sector needs to be developed by providing international linkages for exports, availability of credit through a dedicated SME bank, supply chain efficiencies, adoption of IT, support in R&D and innovation, and a policy support for enhancing the mandate to purchase from SME for large scale projects. Overall goal is to enhance the competitiveness of the SME sector leading to a larger contribution to our economic growth and employment generation.

Cooperative Sector

Every effort will be made to encourage the cooperative sector. BJP commits to review the existing laws with regards to the cooperative sector and will amend the multi-state cooperative act to remove lacunae and anomalies.

Handicrafts

We will move up the value chain of the sector driven by a focus on Quality.

- Market linkages - both national and international.

- Access to credit and information and skills upgradation.

- Value addition will be encouraged through avenues like - branding, packaging and technology.

Artisans

Schemes will be drawn for skills upgradation and enhancement of business opportunities for artisans like smiths, weavers, carpenters, hair-dressers, shoe-smiths, and potters.

Services - Driven by Quality and Efficiency

Business and Trade

The modern era is an era of exchange. Over-regulation needs to be addressed to stop the harassment of the businessmen and traders. At the same time, we have to set up transparent systems, which ensure credibility of our goods and services. At the same time, the bottlenecks in transporting and exporting them have to be removed. Also, the flow of information about our tradable items has to be made available to the rest of the world.

- Focus on Zero defect products.
- Build world class Ports; connecting them with roads and rail to the hinterland so as to drive the maritime trade of the country.
- Air Cargo facilities will be enhanced throughout the country.
- An Export Promotion Mission will be established integrating all stakeholders.
- Current accounts deficit will be brought down aggressively by focusing on exports and reducing the dependency on imports. Value addition on our products will be the biggest task.
- We shall work with the State governments to usher in the GST in an appropriate timeframe. For implementing the same, a robust IT network system will be put in place.
- We will embark on the path of IPRs and Patents in a big way.
- Take all necessary steps to protect the interest of retailers, small traders and small vendors and equip them with the latest techniques and methods to modernize them and make them competitive.
- Commit to ensure that the retailers and SMEs don't have to spend time and money for seeking multiple licenses to start the business. There will a system in place to avoid harassment of small traders.
- Ensure easy availability of institutional credit.
- Review obsolete and multiple laws to reduce and simplify them.

- Remove ambiguity in rules to make way for prompt decisions without any scope for discretion.

- Telecom revolution has touched length and breadth of the country but there is significant scope and necessity to improve the quality of voice and data to fully leverage the potential.

Tourism - Untapped Potential

BJP recognizes the role tourism and hospitality can play as a foreign exchange earner and its ability to create millions of jobs every year. Tourism plays a key role in socio-economic progress through creation of jobs, enterprise, infrastructure development, and foreign exchange earnings.

BJP realizes that the tourism sector needs a clear plan for growth, and BJP commits to initiate a mission mode project to create 50 tourist circuits that are affordable and built around themes like: a.) Archaeological and Heritage, b.) Cultural and Spiritual, c.) Himalayan, d.) Desert, e.) Coastal, f.) Medical (Ayurveda and Modern Medicine), etc. This will lead to creation of infrastructure and employment around each tourist circuit and help in boosting revenue generation.

Specialized course in tourism will be started for capacity development. Safety and Security of tourists would be accorded due priority.

Labour Force - The Pillar of Our Growth

BJP recognizes the fact that the labour is the key to the revival of the economy and so are the laws governing them. We believe in promoting a harmonious relationship between labour and the industry with both playing an important contributory role in economic growth and development.

We will ensure that the interests of labour in the unorganized sector are protected.

For the organized labour, we propose to encourage industry owners and labour to embrace the concept of 'Industry Family'. This concept, in which industry owners and labours bond as a family, is guided by the principles of efficiency, skill development and upgradation, productivity, appropriate wages and perquisites, and security towards this end.

We will:

- Issue identity cards to the unorganized sector labourers and arrangements will be made to provide them good quality health and education services. Also, their skills will be upgraded through appropriate training programs.
- Extend access to modern financial services to labour - including considering the option of setting up a dedicated Workers Bank.
- Bring together all stakeholders to review our Labour laws which are outdated, complicated and even contradictory.
- Strengthen the Pension and Health Insurance safety nets for all kinds of labourers.

Housing - No Longer a Mirage

We will roll out a massive Low cost Housing programme to ensure that by the time the nation completes 75 years of its Independence, every family will have a pucca house of its own. It will be an innovatively designed scheme that dovetails various existing programmes and also encourages the housing sector by appropriate policy interventions and credit availability including interest subventions, where necessary.

Our proposed programme will further ensure that these houses are equipped with the basic facilities of toilet, piped water supply, electricity and proper Access.

To do this we will, amongst others:

- Prioritize all our resources towards this goal.
- Leverage on land as a resource in urban areas and demand for unskilled labour in the rural areas.
- Innovatively structure the programme to converge and dovetail various existing programmes, while adding the missing links.
- Simultaneously encourage the overall housing sector, through appropriate policy interventions and credit availability and interest subvention schemes.

Physical Infrastructure - Better than the Best

India should no longer be limited by its infrastructure. In fact, we have to create robust infrastructure, which drives growth. For this purpose, we have to devote ourselves for a decade. We have to think big. Also, looking to the expansion in our population as well as social and economic activities, we have to build our infrastructure in a futuristic way. Growth of this sector means the growth of cement, steel, electricity and many other associated industries and directly leads to massive job creation.

To achieve this, we will take following steps.

- Work on the Freight Corridors and attendant Industrial Corridors will be expedited. This will result in the faster movement of people and goods.

- Remote states like those in the Northeast and Jammu and Kashmir will be connected with the rest of India through world class highways and rail lines.

- National Highway construction projects will be expedited, especially Border and Coastal highways.

- Every village will be connected through all-weather roads.

- We shall modernize existing and operational Airports and build new ones especially connecting smaller towns and all tourism circuits. In addition, there is a potential for inland air transportation to various remote and local locations in the country. Such air strips will be developed so that low cost air travelling becomes possible within the country.

- We will evolve an economic model of Port-led development. India is blessed with a long coastline.

We will modernize existing ports on one hand, and develop new ones on the other - stringing together our Sagar Mala project.

- Public Private Partnership would be encouraged to tap into private sector resources as well as expertise. An institutional framework would be established for the same; while regulators would be given greater autonomy as well as accountability.

Next Generation Infrastructure

We will:

- Set up Gas Grids to make gas available to households and industry.

- Set up a National Optical-Fibre Network up to the village level; and Wi-Fi zones in public areas.

- harness our advanced satellite technology and expertise for development.

Transport

The BJP realizes the importance of travel for the vibrancy of the economy and social unity.

BJP will:

- Create a public transport system, which can reduce the dependence on personal vehicles for transport, thereby, reducing cost, time to travel as well as ecological cost.

- Launch an Integrated Public transport project which will include roadways, railways and waterways.

- Develop waterways for passenger and cargo transport.

- Develop National logistics network for faster movement of goods.

Railway

Indian Railways is the lifeline of the country. It will be modernized, strengthened and upgraded to serve passengers as well as the country's economy. This will be done in a planned manner focusing on national development, rather than political exigency.

- Hinterland will be connected to the ports through strategic new Rail networks.

- Agri Rail network will be established with Train Wagons designed to cater to the specific needs of perishable Agricultural products like milk and vegetables as well as light weight wagons for salt movement.

- Tourist Rail, including Pilgrimage Rail.

- Railways Modernization, inducting of state-of-the-art technology.

- Special focus on developing skilled human resources to meet future demand.

- Prioritize Safety and invest in long required overhaul of stressed infrastructure, strict norms and warning systems.

- Modernize and equip all stations with requisite infrastructure and public utilities.

- Convert all unmanned crossings into manned crossings in a phased manner.

- Initiate R&D for indigenous railways, coach design and signals.

- We will launch Diamond Quadrilateral project of High Speed Train network (bullet train).

Water - Make It Reach to All Homes, Farms and Factories

Trends indicate that India would be a 'water stressed' state by 2050, and the gap between the demand and supply would be 50%. BJP recognizes the seriousness of the issue. Also, most importantly, potable drinking water is not available to the entire population despite more than six decades of independence. Water is a dwindling resource with the threat of water scarcity looming large. We will address this in a comprehensive manner across multiple dimensions. BJP remains committed to giving high priority to water security.

- Launch the 'Pradhan Mantri Gram Sinchayee Yojana' with a motto of 'har khet ko paani'. We will launch multi-pronged 'water strategy' for reducing farmer's dependence on monsoon. Increase irrigated land by completing the long pending irrigation projects on priority.

- We will nurture ground water recharge harnessing rain water to reduce dependence on ground water.

- Encourage efficient use, water conservation, recycling and rain water harvesting.

- Sewage treatment plants to prevent the pollution of rivers.

- Desalination plants for drinking water supply in coastal cities.

- Inter-linking of rivers based on feasibility.

- Examination of ground water to eliminate toxic chemicals, particularly arsenic and fluorides. To ensure drinking water security to all.

We will:

- Encourage setting up of drinking water supply grid in water scarce areas.

- Promote decentralized, demand-driven, community-managed water resource management, water supply and environmental sanitation.

- Facilitate piped water to all households.

Energy - Generate More, Use Rationally, Waste Less

BJP realizes the need to focus on generation and distribution of power as a national security issue, so that the growth is not negatively impacted due to supply issues in the energy sector. The overarching goal of energy security is to ensure affordable energy for various consumer segments. Steps will be taken to avoid over-dependence on any one fuel and ensure supplier diversity, to avoid reliance on one supplier, country and developing indigenous capacities to meet the emerging needs.

BJP will:

- Come out with a responsible and comprehensive 'National Energy Policy'.

- Focus on development of energy infrastructure, human resource development and upgradation of technology.

- Take steps to maximize the potential of oil, gas, hydel power, ocean, wind, coal and nuclear sources. BJP considers energy efficiency and conservation crucial to energy security.

- Set up small-hydro power generation projects to harness the hydropower that is not being used at the moment. Small projects can be set up with local support and without displacement of the local population.

- Take Steps to increase the domestic coal exploration and production, to bridge the demand and supply gap. Oil and gas explorations would also be expedited in the country. This will also help to reduce the import bill.

- Give a thrust to renewable sources of energy as an important component of India's energy mix.

- Expand and strengthen the national solar mission.

Science and Technology - India Innovates and India Leads

India has been a knowledge economy and has been a leader in science and technology from the ancient times. India now needs policies and programs to reclaim its global leadership position in science and technology. BJP recognizes the need to create an ecosystem for fundamental research and innovation, keeping the objective of science with a human face in the service of the common man. Science and technology has enormous potential to bridge the disparities between the urban and rural India, rich and poor. Scientific education and technology needs to be encouraged, promoted, practiced and leveraged with renewed vision and vigour.

BJP recognizes the central role of science and technology in raising the quality of life of the people of the country, particularly of the disadvantaged sections of society in creating wealth for all, in making India globally competitive, in utilizing natural resources in a sustainable manner, in protecting the environment and ensuring national security. We will also encourage and incentivize private sector investments - both domestic and foreign, in science and technology and in high-end research aimed towards innovation.

We will focus on the following:

- Ensuring food, agricultural, nutritional and environmental, wealth, health and energy security of the people on a sustainable basis, using science and technology.

- Mounting a direct and sustained effort on the alleviation of poverty, enhancing livelihood security, removal of hunger and malnutrition, reduction of drudgery and regional imbalances, both rural and urban, and generation of employment, by using scientific and technological capabilities along with our traditional knowledge pool.

- Encouraging research and innovation in areas of relevance for the economy and society, particularly by promoting close and productive interaction between private and public institutions. Sectors such as agriculture (particularly soil, water management, human and animal nutrition and fisheries), water, health, and education, and industry, energy including renewable energy, communication and transportation would be accorded highest priority. Leveraging of technologies such as information technology, biotechnology and material sciences would be done with special importance.

- Encouraging research and application to meet the challenges of climate change and for forecasting, prevention and mitigation of natural hazards, particularly floods, cyclones, earthquakes, drought and landslides.

- Promoting international science and technology cooperation towards achieving the goals of national development and security and making it a key element of our international relations.

- Devise schemes, programs and opportunities to encourage the youth to take scientific research and innovation as a career.

- Provide work environment and professional opportunities in fundamental scientific research, to make research careers more appealing, so that the nation can harness the best of brains for scientific research leading to enhancing the national productivity and competitiveness and reverse brain drain.

- Build world class, regional centres of excellence of scientific research in the field of nanotechnology, material sciences, thorium technology and brain research.

- Create an ecosystem for multi-country and inter-disciplinary collaborative research and establish an Intellectual Property Rights Regime which maximizes the incentive for generation and protection of intellectual property for all type of inventors.

- Achieving synergy between industry and scientific research. Autonomous technology transfer organizations will be created as associate organizations of universities and national laboratories to transfer the know-how generated by them to industry. Industry will be encouraged to adopt or support educational and research institutions to help direct science and technology endeavours towards tangible industrial goals.

- Promotion of innovation by creating a comprehensive national system of innovation.

- Indigenous knowledge, based on our long and rich tradition will be further developed and harnessed for the purpose of wealth and employment generation

- To promote science popularization schemes extensively.

- Bring the changes in secondary education to focus on application of science.

- Set an institute of Big data and Analytics for studying the impact of big data across sectors for predictive science.

- To do research for the eradication of tropical diseases.

- Establish institutes of Technology for Rural Development.

- Establish a Central University dedicated to Himalayan Technology.

- Promote research and application of nuclear science in medicines, industry and agriculture.

Flora, Fauna and Environment - Safeguarding Our Tomorrow

The present generation has to make this world a better place to live. A better place not only for us, but for our future generations as well. We have to nurture the environment, institutions, people, resources and amenities. We have to combine the past, the present and the future. We have to have a holistic view of human life for sustainable development.

We have to develop the assets and amenities for ourselves in a manner that leaves an equally good or even better environment for the future generations. We will put sustainability at the centre of our thoughts and actions, working on the principle that inclusive growth cannot be limited by the barriers of time and space - it has to be built on the foundations of the past, leverage on the opportunities of the present, and preserve and enhance its resources for the future. We will take Climate Change mitigation initiatives with all seriousness and work with the global community and institutions in this regard.

We will:

- Encourage Cleaner production.

- Cleaner fuels will be promoted so as to bring down the pollution levels particularly in the cities.

- The concept of pro-active 'Carbon Credit' will be promoted.

- Ecological Audit of projects and pollution indexing of cities and townships will be done on scientific basis.

- Pollution control mechanisms will be set up on priority basis.

- In addition to protecting the existing forests and wildlife reserves, the wastelands of the country will be used for social forestry.

- Guidelines for Green buildings and energy efficient work places will be brought out.

- R&D and Human Resource Development in Environment Technology will be promoted.

- Set up fool proof mechanisms for protection and preservation of wild life.

- Encourage citizen's participation in reforestation, agro-forestry and social forestry, through targeted programmes.

- Encourage and incentivize innovative garbage disposal and waste management practices, especially recycling techniques.

The Himalayas

BJP is committed to serious endeavours for creating a global awareness regarding the conservation of Himalayas and will take the following steps:

- Launch 'National Mission on Himalayas' as a unique programme of inter-governmental partnership, in coordinated policy making and capacity building across states and sectors.

- Create a 'Himalayan Sustainability Fund'.

- Create a Central University dedicated to the Himalayan Technology.

- Give due Importance to the programmes devised to arrest the melting of Himalayan glaciers from which most of the rivers in North India originate.

Natural & National Resources - Use When Required, Protect Where Necessary

Indian belief has been best encapsulated in Gandhiji's words that "there is enough for everyone's need, but not for everyone's greed". Need is not the issue. Greed is. A country's progress depends upon its resources and how they are harnessed and protected. Those in power have to realize they are just trustees of the resources of the nation. The resources are neither meant for them nor for their masters. If we bring this basic shift in thinking of the Government, which Mahatma Gandhi also advocated, all problems will be resolved.

In recent years, it has been noticed that country's tangible and intangible resources have been looted with impunity. The adverse result is being felt on two sides: Firstly, the proceeds of the resources have not gone to the public exchequer. Secondly, because of this culture of usurping, the same resources are not available for public purposes. The management of natural resources is marred with either misappropriation or misallocation. This has to be set right.

- We will set in place national policies on critical natural resources like coal, minerals, spectrum, etc. - spelling out in black and white how much should be utilized at what time and pace; how this should be strategically phased out to ensure sustainability; who should be allotted what responsibility of extraction and at what cost.

- State Governments will be taken into confidence for harnessing of these resources.

- We will implement auction of precious resources through efficient mechanisms including e- auction.

- Resource mapping, exploration and management will be undertaken through the use of technology.

- Value addition will be encouraged in all resources, instead of just marketing.

Secure Indians - Zero Tolerance on Terrorism, Extremism and Crime

Comprehensive national security is not just about borders, but in its broad terms includes military security; economic security; cyber security; energy, food and water and health security; and social cohesion and harmony. To effectively address the issues of national security, we need to address the issues of - human resources, science and technology, system of governance and money.

National security cannot be compartmentalized based on one of issues but needs a clear roadmap to address it. Over the past decade, lack of a strong and visionary leadership, coupled with multiple power centres, has failed to address the issue of national security, leading to a chaotic situation and denting India's image in the international arena.

India has a sensitive neighbourhood and there are internal security issues. There have been intrusions inside the LAC (Line of actual control), loss of squadrons of combat aircraft by the air force, witnessing of a series of accidents by the Navy, leading to a loss in its combating capability built over many decades, communal riots, Maoist attacks, increase in incidence of Pakistan backed terror groups in India, illegal immigration across the eastern border, and racists' attacks in the national capital. All these are indications of surrendering of India's interest. This calls for a review and overhauling of the current system. With the financial situation worsening, the issue of national security can acquire a horrifying dimension.

BJP recognizes the importance of identifying a clear roadmap to address the issue head-on, with radical systemic changes.

Internal Security

BJP will:

- Revive the anti-terror mechanism that has been dismantled by the Congress, strengthen the role of NIA and put a system in place for swift and fair trial of terror related cases.

- Reform the National Security Council to make it the hub of all sector-related assessments. It will be accountable for real-time intelligence dissemination. Digital and Cyber security will be a thrust area.

- Insulate intelligence agencies from political intervention and interference.

- Completely revamp the intelligence gathering system by modernizing the intelligence department.

- Provide the State governments with all assistance to modernize their respective police forces and equip them with the latest technology. This will be taken up on a mission mode approach.

- Strengthen and expand the Civil Defence and Home Guards mechanism to create a group of citizens for community defence, self-defence and disaster management.

- Encourage and strengthen NCC training at the college and University level.

- Chalk a national plan in consultation and participation of the state Governments, to address the challenges posed by the Maoist's insurgency. Talks with the insurgent groups will be conditional and within the framework of the constitution.

– Take urgent steps for the safety of the migrant workers and communities from the Northeast and other states.

External Security - Its Boundary, Beauty and Bounty

BJP will:

- Address the issue of reforms with regards to defence equipment, support services, organizational reforms and other related matters.

- Address the increasing shortage of commissioned and non-commissioned staff in the defence forces on a priority basis, in a time bound manner.

- Implement one rank, one pension.

- Build a War Memorial to recognize and honour the gallantry of our soldiers.

- Take measures to make Short Service Commission more attractive.

- Set up the National Maritime Authority which will be equipped with the best of infrastructure, and will focus on coastal security.

- Modernize armed forces, and increase the R&D in defence, with a goal of developing indigenous defence technologies and fast tracking of defence purchases.

- Deal with cross border terrorism with a firm hand.

- Review and improve the border management. Punitive measures will be introduced to check illegal immigration.

- Set up four dedicated defence universities to meet the shortage of manpower.

- Appoint a Veterans Commission to address the grievances of veterans, including reforming ECHS and re-employment of ex-servicemen.

- Ensure greater participation of Armed Forces in the decision-making process of the Ministry of Defence.

- Implement measures to improve the efficiency of Armed Forces Tribunals, and minimize appeals by the Government.

- Ensure that servicemen can register and vote from their place of posting.

- Initiate the process of digitization of defence land in cantonment and in other places.

Defence Production

With its skilled human resources and technical talent, India can emerge as a global platform for defence hardware manufacture and software production. BJP will strengthen the Defence Research and Development Organization (DRDO); encourage private sector participation and investment, including FDI in selected defence industries.

- Technology transfer in defence manufacturing will be encouraged to the maximum.
- We will find solutions to the problems hampering the growth of the defence sector.
- We will encourage domestic industry to have a larger share in design and production of military hardware and platforms for both domestic use and exports, in a competitive environment.

Independent Strategic Nuclear Programme

BJP believes that the strategic gains acquired by India during the Atal Bihari Vajpayee regime on the nuclear programme have been frittered away by the Congress. Our emphasis was, and remains on the beginning of a new thrust on framing policies that would serve India's national interest in the 21st century. We will follow a two-pronged independent nuclear programme, unencumbered by foreign pressure and influence, for civilian and military purposes, especially as nuclear power is a major contributor to India's energy sector.

BJP will:

- Study in detail India's nuclear doctrine, and revise and update it, to make it relevant to challenges of current times.
- Maintain a credible minimum deterrent that is in tune with changing geostatic realities.
- Invest in India's indigenous Thorium Technology Programme.

Foreign Relations - Nation First, Universal Brotherhood

BJP believes a resurgent India must get its rightful place in the comity of nations and international institutions. The vision is to fundamentally reboot and reorient the foreign policy goals, content and process, in a manner that locates India's global strategic engagement in a new paradigm and on a wider canvass, that is not just limited to political diplomacy, but also includes our economic, scientific, cultural, political and security interests, both regional and global, on the principles of equality and mutuality, so that it leads to an economically stronger India and its voice is heard in the international fora.

BJP believes that political stability, progress and peace in the region are essential for south Asia's growth and development. The Congress-led UPA has failed to establish enduring friendly and cooperative relations with India's neighbours. India's relations with traditional allies have turned cold. India and its neighbours have drifted apart. Instead of clarity, we have seen confusion. The absence of statecraft has never been felt so acutely as today. India is seen to be floundering, whereas it should have been engaging with the world with confidence. The collapse of the Indian economy has contributed to the sorry state of foreign affairs in no small measure.

We will build a strong, self-reliant and self-confident India, regaining its rightful place in the comity of nations. In this, we will be firstly guided by our centuries old tradition of 'Vasudhaiv Kutumbkam' The whole world is my family. At the same time, our foreign policy will be based on best National interests. We will create a web of allies to mutually further our interests. We will leverage all our resources and people to play a greater role on the international high table.

India has long failed to duly appreciate the full extent and gamut of its soft power potential. There is a need to integrate our soft power avenues into our external interchange, particularly, harnessing and focusing on the spiritual, cultural and philosophical dimensions of it. India has always played a major role in world affairs, offering a lot to the World. This has been its tradition since time immemorial. The magnetic power of India has always been in its ancient wisdom and heritage, elucidating principles like harmony and equity. This continues to be equally relevant to the world today in today's times of Soft power. We will adopt Proactive Diplomacy to spread the same. India was reckoned not only as Vishwaguru but also a vibrant trading society. Our ancestors used to trade with foreign nations through the routes of sea, centuries ago. This was based on the strength of our business acumen and integrity, our products and crafts. The symbols of our ancient civilizations stand as a testimony to our architectural and urban planning excellence. We will revive Brand India with the help of our strengths of 5 T's: Tradition, Talent, Tourism, Trade and Technology.

Guiding Principles of our Foreign Policy will be:

- Equations will be mended through pragmatism and a doctrine of mutually beneficial and interlocking relationships, based on enlightened national interest.
- We will champion uniform international opinion on issues like Terrorism and Global Warming.
- Instead of being led by big power interests, we will engage proactively on our own with countries in the neighbourhood and beyond.
- In our neighbourhood we will pursue friendly relations. However, where required we will not hesitate from taking strong stand and steps.
- We will work towards strengthening Regional forums like SAARC and ASEAN.
- We will continue our dialogue, engagement and cooperation, with global forums like BRICS, G20, IBSA, SCO and ASEM. States will be encouraged to play a greater role in diplomacy; actively building relations with foreign countries to harness their mutual cultural and commercial strengths.

Also,

- We will expand and empower our pool of diplomats, ensuring our message is taken to the world and our great nation represented on the whole in a befitting manner.
- The NRIs, PIOs and professionals settled abroad are a vast reservoir to articulate the national interests and affairs globally. This resource will be harnessed for strengthening Brand India.
- India shall remain a natural home for persecuted Hindus and they shall be welcome to seek refuge here.

Cultural Heritage

Ram Mandir: BJP reiterates its stand to explore all possibilities within the framework of the constitution to facilitate the construction of the Ram Temple in Ayodhya.

Ram Setu: Ram Setu is a part of our cultural heritage and also of strategic importance due to its vast thorium deposits. These facts will be taken into consideration while taking any decision on 'Sethu- Samudram Channel' project.

Ganga: River Ganga is a symbol of faith in India and has a special place in the Indian psyche. It is Mukti dayini. In addition, it is also Jivan dayini for the parts of the country it flows. People and cattle depend on it for agriculture, fodder and drinking water. Pure water of the Ganga is thus essential for the spiritual as well as physical wellbeing of India.

Unfortunately, however, even after decades of independence, the Ganga continues to be polluted and is drying. BJP commits to ensure the cleanliness, purity and uninterrupted flow of the Ganga on priority. In addition, a massive 'Clean Rivers Programme' will be launched across the country driven by people's participation.

Cow and its Progeny: In view of the contribution of cow and its progeny to agriculture, socio-economic and cultural life of our country, the Department of Animal Husbandry will be suitably strengthened and empowered for the protection and promotion of cow and its progeny.

- Necessary legal framework will be created to protect and promote cow and its progeny.

- A National Cattle Development board will be set up to implement a Programme for the improvement of indigenous livestock breeds.

Heritage Sites: We will provide appropriate resources for the maintenance and restoration of all national heritage sites, and to prevent their vandalisation in any form. The digitization of archives and archaeological and musicological records would be initiated. A National Mission for beautifying and improving the infrastructure and amenities at pilgrimage centres of all faiths will be launched.

Languages: Indian Languages are repositories of our rich literature, history, culture, art and scientific achievements. Many of our dialects are important source for knowing our heritage. BJP would promote Indian languages, and put measures for the development of all Indian languages, so that they become a powerful vehicle for creating a knowledge society.

Uniform Civil Code

Article 44 of the constitution of India lists Uniform Civil Code as one of the Directive Principles of state policy. BJP believes that there cannot be gender equality till such time India adopts a Uniform Civil Code, which protects the rights of all women, and the BJP reiterates its stand to draft a Uniform Civil Code, drawing upon the best traditions and harmonizing them with the modern times.

Conclusion - Amritmay Bharat

We aim to build a modern, prosperous and vibrant India - Ek Bharat, Shreshtha Bharat, based on our ethos and values. We have to convert ourselves into a knowledge based society and economy, powered by experience, tools of technology and energy of our people. BJP commits itself to this task and promises to work relentlessly towards this goal, for which we are seeking sixty months.

In 2022, we will be celebrating 75 years of India's Independence. In Indian culture, this is celebrated as Amrit Mahotsav. For us, every day and every step, every journey and every process will be dedicated to make Amritmay Bharat. And all this will be done by all of us, for all of us!

This is not the time to sit back. This is the time when each of us has to get up and contribute our might to bring the change.

Let's come together, vote BJP to make Ek Bharat, Shreshtha Bharat.

Jai Hind!

The election manifesto of BJP is the manifesto of the nation. Future alone can tell is how many of the promises made here have actually been fulfilled by BJP.

Social Media and Modi

The results of Parliamentary elections polls proved that the election was fought on social media instead of print and electronic media and the social media won this contest. It is being said repeatedly that this media made Modi, hero of the campaign. Right from the prime time on TV channels to front pages of newspapers, it was Modi all along but I refute the conclusion that Modi was made the hero by the media. In fact, Modi became a brand and the media found this more saleable. Therefore, the media spared no effort in selling this brand. Media needs a brand to sell from time to time. Remember those days when media was projecting the Vice President of Congress Rahul Gandhi also as a media brand. Recall the 2009 Parliamentary elections when he talked of leading the youth of the nation and took the centre stage in the prime time of every news channel and front page of every newspaper. At that time nobody raised the objection that all of it was sponsored.

In fact, it is a matter of concern that whenever a brand starts to sell in the market and also if it has a lot of customers, then it is often said that a lot of money has been spent on advertisement and publicity. But this is the demand of the market. TV channels earn their TRP also from these brands. Try to recall Anna Hazare's agitation against corruption when all the news from the TV channels had vanished and one unit of the media was standing by round the clock in Ramlila Grounds. At that time, nobody thought that all of it was sponsored but now when Narendra Modi has been given a slot of prime time, then everyone wants to prove that all this is sponsored. I do not want to go into the reasoning behind this. All I want to mention that the parliamentary election is a win for the social media which created a brand out of Modi. By sending just one tweet in a day, it is not easy to get TRP. Millions of people tweet every day but they are meaningless tweets. Whereas when Narendra Modi tweets, he is showered with criticism.

We were talking about the victory of social media. In fact, Narendra Modi understood its true power and in order to use it he laid its foundation as early as two years before the elections with the aim to create a facilitating climate for the party by use of social media. To achieve this, a full-fledged team was constituted and he recruited all those professionals who understood the finer points and nitty-gritties of social media. Along with this, he got closer to bloggers also who put across their opinion through their blogs. He formally met the bloggers in Ahmedabad and tried to understand their opinion as to how he could have a firmer grip on social media. It is very clear that he has always considered social media as a very powerful weapon and he used this weapon with great finesse and skill. It is not that parties like Congress had not understood the pulse of this medium but due to their lack of foresightedness, they could not achieve what Modi could.

During the Parliamentary elections of 2009, both Congress and BJP had set up their war rooms and in this election, the war room of Congress was stronger that BJP with the result that Congress could score a major victory. This time Congress was left far behind and BJP scored a victory. The reason was very clear. Modi knew that if he had to ensure victory in the elections of 2014, he must capture the social media. To achieve this, he established his grip on all social media like Twitter and Facebook and by mustering financial resources he was successful to plough in new bloggers and Facebook users on his side. This is the reason that all the websites were inundated with the slogan 'Abki bar Modi Sarkar'. His opponents might allege that enormous amount of money was spent but I would like to know which political party does not. Did Congress not possess financial muscle and did other parties like BSP, SP, RKP, or DMK not have funds? AAP party gathered such tremendous strength by using social media in the Delhi elections that all other regional parties looked dwarfed before it. Committed party workers of AAP did not only spread their party's policies through social media but they also exposed cases of rampant corruption.

One can estimate the growing power of social media by this fact that not only many countries in the world have banned social networking sites but many organisations also have put restrictions on their use in their workplaces so that there is no disturbance in their working. The media analysts may claim that social media does not pose much threat in the country but the way, in which information revolution has taken place, the power of social media has grown very fast. The number of Facebook users has increased multifold in far-flung places making it very powerful and widespread.

Twitter has about 35 lakh fans of Modi and he is the number one Indian politician on this media. Under the guise of active participation in social media, he has created his own place in mainstream media also. He is the first Indian leader who has used google hangout for group video chat. Around 82,000 participants from 116 countries saw the direct transmission of this hangout session through You tube. During this video chat session there were 70, 000 tweets for Modi and his website had 1, 66,000 hits. During this election, by use of social media and new techniques of public contact, BJP left all the other competitors far behind. The BJP page of Facebook got 45 lakh 'like' whereas Congress could muster only 33 lakhs. Social media is a two edged weapon and Modi made enormously effective use of this weapon in the general elections. Modi has created a new segment of fans through the social media. He not only consistently expresses his opinions on the social media but he also establishes a dialogue with people and the result was that the young generation which wanted to express their opinions through the social media became his fans. At the end of ninth and the last phase of elections, Modi immediately thanked, in fact within minutes, through Tweet, his voters, Election Commission and social media. This kind of alertness demonstrated by Modi only points towards the fact that the power and influence of social media is bound to increase in the coming days.

Challenges before NaMo

Narendra Modi has now become the Prime Minister but he confronted with a mounted of challenges. These challenges of course pertain to peoples' expectations but they also include how to accelerate the speed of progress, how to get relief from price-rise and corruption and similar critical issues bothering the nation. It is true that the pace of progress has retarded. On the surface, we see people who own houses, cars and many other luxuries but even today, serious problems like inflation and unemployment are engulfing millions of people. During his election rallies, Modi has already said that the growth rate of the economy is in fact less than 5 percent. Under such circumstances, the biggest challenge would be how to double the growth rate. If the growth rate increases, we will get relief from problems like inflation and unemployment. Every section of the society has been badly affected by the ill-effects of inflation. The entire nation was troubled by the increased inflation rate during UPA regime. Leaders in Congress also accepted that the rising prices had tarnished the image of the party and this became a major issue for the BJP which they used against Congress. Inflation has shot up to 8 percent. To accelerate the rate of development and growth and to step adequate measures to contain inflation is the foremost challenge for Modi government. The new Government also faces the challenge of banking sector which is passing through tremendous financial crisis. Companies are unable to repay their loans because of the present economic conditions. There are ten major industrial houses in India which are facing a lot of difficulties in repaying the interest alone. They owe huge sums of money to the lending banks. Since they are not getting back the money they have lent as loan, seven major banks are under pressure. Union bank of India had almost got liquidated. It was saved by pumping in almost two thousand crore rupees. As a matter of fact, a policy of recapitalization was adopted during the tenure of Finance Minister P. Chidambaram. All this has resulted in pushing the banking sector in a major crisis. The share of Government in these banks has gone upto almost 80 percent.

Therefore, reforms in banking sector are a major challenge. Only when inflation is brought under control with good treasury management, Reserve Bank of India can reduce the lending rates which in turn will encourage more investment and thus the economy can be brought back on track. Another major challenge confronting this Government is that it has only six weeks to prepare the central budget which it must present before end of June. The new Finance Minister will have to handle a plethora problems pertaining to economic system.

Currency market has hopes that Modi will extend full cooperation to Reserve Bank of India to regulate the exchange rate of rupee against US dollar. In the last two years we have faced two kinds of scenarios. Either the rupee gets very strong which puts exporters into trouble and their profits go down. On the contrary when it gets weak, imports become very expensive. Exchange rate of rupee is a very big challenge for the RBI Governor Raghuraman Rajan. Under such circumstances, businessmen expect that the new Government will cooperate with RBI. Similarly scandals, scams and corruption have been tarnishing the image of UPA government. Scandals after scandals have not only spoilt the reputation of the Government but they have also pushed back the development and progress of the nation.

The people of India expect Narendra Modi to free the country from corruption and broaden the path to progress. The youth of the nation are confronted with unemployment as a major challenge. They are brilliant and innovative but their talent does not have an outlet. Every field is fraught with tremendous challenges and crises. The youth of the country have put their faith in the new Government hoping that they will get some opportunities through more jobs. Out of the total population, 28 crores are young. They need more options of employment. They look forward to better climate enabling them to get ahead in life. They need better facilities. Narendra Modi constituted a special investigating force as soon as he became the Prime Minister to bring the black money back into the country. Black money worth more than 25 lakh crores rupees is deposited in overseas banks. If it can be brought back, it will make a major contribution to the development of the nation.

Safety of women poses a major challenge to the newly formed Government. Crimes towards women have seen an alarming increase in India. There is an outcry in the minds of common citizens which is justified. The manner in which people came on the street in the Nirbhaya episode represents their sentiments. The new Government will have to take strong and immediate steps so that women feel safe both within the four walls of their home as well as outside on the street. Apart from ensuring strict compliance of laws, the new Government will have to work on changing the mindset of people towards women. BJP has been advocating for simplification of tax structure in the state since a very long period. A lot needs to be done in the direction of tax reforms. Goods and service tax and direct tax code are also included in this. Government will have debate this very thoroughly. In addition, the problems of terrorism, infiltration, ending Naxalism, free the parliament from criminals are major challenges for the Government. Internal party rivalries and to get cooperation from alliance parties is a major task before Narendra Modi.

When Narendra Modi became the Prime Minister of the nation, media defined the challenges before him in the following words. Navbharat Times said, "Narendra Modi took oath as the fifteenth Prime Minister of the country and brightened the image of the Government. This was the most golden moment of his amazing climb on the ladder of success. With this starts the test of his fulfilling the ambitions of millions of his countrymen. The people of this nation have selected him to give this test. On the occasion of the start of the journey of this Government which is a creation of peoples' aspirations, we would like to remind them of all the promises they made during the campaign and assure ourselves

–'Acche din aane wale hai'." Hindustan Times said, "The task of changing the face of nation's politics, which Congress could not accomplished has been achieved by Narendra Modi." Nai Duniya wrote, "This is the first experiment how a single individual can influence the outcome and how the entire population of the country put all their hopes in him. Now it is necessary that the experiment should succeed and if it does, it would change the entire profile of South Asia." Most newspapers analyzed his win and challenges before him in a similar manner.

The second cabinet meeting of Prime Minister Modi's Government was held on 29th May. He has clarified the top ten priorities of the Government to his cabinet.

Top ten priorities

1. **Morale of the administrators**: Build up confidence in Bureaucracy so that there is no fear to face any consequences and they will be able to implement the policies.

2. **To welcome innovative ideas** and babus will be given freedom to work. Be it an officer or common man, all can give their suggestions for creation of a superior India (Shreshtha Bharat).Ministers should ask the opinions of people on Facebook and Twitter. Officers should prepare a blue print of their pan and contact either the PM or his Minister.

3. **To focus on education, health, water, energy and roads** will be a priority. If these basic necessities are not fulfilled, how can you think of India as a developed nation? Therefore, the Government will have to provide education, health-schemes in each town and village, clean drinking water, water for irrigation and roads for easy transportation to all on top priority.

4. **To ensure transparency in the government** and promote E-Auction in tendering government work. Corruption is a matter of great worry for the entire country and efforts for its eradication must start at the top. Every policy and every action of the new Government must be transparent.

5. **System will be placed to manage the inter-ministerial issues.** File from one Ministry is held up in another. This results in stalling of work and results in allegations and counter-allegations. To eliminate this, there will be a new system of inter-ministry coordination.

6. **People oriented system will be in placed in government machinery to fulfil the mandate**. You can win over the voters and gain their mandate by fulfilling the promises in your mandate and

manifesto. They have to be kept up in a timely manner. Therefore the promises made in the manifesto, policies enumerated in it and the results achieved must be continuously monitored.

7. **Addressing concerns relating to economy.** Hopes of the nation are very large and they continue to get bigger. If there is no drop in rate of inflation and prices do not come down, then opportunities of employment will not increase. The health of GDP will not improve. Economy must be brought back on the track by making improvements at the policy level and accelerating the pace of development. If this is not done, there will be frustration all around.

8. **Infrastructural and investment reforms**. We will have to emphasise on attracting investments to bring back the economy on track. We will have to remove the roadblocks. We will also reform the policies to prevent pilferage of resources and to ensure their optimum utilisation.

9. **Implement policies in a time bound manner.** Plans are made but they get lost in the jungle of red-tapism. It is important that there should be a deadline for every task and responsibility and accountability of who is answerable must be fixed. If we use the Corporate parlance, we must emphasize on timely delivery.

10. **Maintain stability and sustainability in government policy.** Whether it is an overseas investor or bureaucracy, everyone is worried about the change of Government or when would the policies of the Government take a U turn. This is not a good sign. Not only should the Government policies be clear but there should be a longevity and continuity in them so that the vision behind these policies is clear to everybody.

When one looks at the above ten priorities, it is not difficult to understand just at one glance at them that BJP government is much different than others. They are seriously aware of the promises made by them and their views are simple and straight-forward. It is also a fact that to implement them is not at all an easy task but since the Prime Minister is personally prepared monitor them, there is no reason why they should not be successfully fulfilled. We may have to wait for some time for their success but it is evident that this philosophy and the plans are unique and unprecedented. By treading on this path, the nation can reach a new realm of development and progress.

A positive beginning

After he took charge of the office of Prime Minister and thus taking the reins of the country in his hands, he delivered a positive message when he said that he is serious about the issues based on which the country has voted him to power. Therefore his first decision was to get back the black money deposited in various banks abroad. To do this, he constituted an SIT (Special Investigation Team) and put the mission on fast track.

The Chairman and Deputy Chairman of the SIT are retired Supreme Court judges whereas it will be assisted by the revenue secretary, directors of CBI, IB, RAW and ED, the CBDT chairman and an RBI deputy governor. The matter of black money was brought up by the famous lawyer Ram Jethmalani in a Public Interest Litigation.

The Supreme Court had already given a directive to constitute a Special Investigating Team as early as 3 years back on 4th July, 2011 but because of the obstinacy of UPA Government, SIT could not be constituted. UPA Government kept on fighting a case against the constitution of SIT for 3 years in the Supreme Court. In the end, on 1st May, Supreme Court cancelled the petition of UPA and gave a firm directive to constitute SIT.

After Justice Jeevan Reddy expressed his inability to become the Chairman of the committee, the honorary Court asked for the reconstitution of SIT and appointed retired judge Mr M B Shah as a Chairman and retired judge Mr Arijit Pasayat as the Vice-Chairman. They will be assisted by the revenue secretary, directors of CBI, IB, RAW and ED, the CBDT chairman and an RBI deputy governor. SIT will not only investigate against the people who have black money in India but also those Indians who have deposited black money in overseas banks.

The honorary Court had already made it clear that SIT can once again investigate against the biggest culprit of black money crimes Hassan Ali and his accomplice Taparia. The SIT has been charged with the responsibility and duties of investigation, initiation of proceedings and prosecution in cases of Hasan Ali and other matters involving unaccounted money. The panel will have jurisdiction in cases where investigations have commenced. The SIT will also prepare a comprehensive action plan, including creation of an institutional structure that could enable the country to fight the battle against unaccounted money. It should report on the status of its work to the court from time to time which are pending, are waiting to be initiated or have been completed. This will ensure that black money cannot be transferred into overseas banks. SIT will work under the directions of Supreme Court and report to it regarding the progress in the matter of menace of black money from time to time through a report.

Along with this, Modi also gave a ten point programme for 'Good days' and the concerned Ministers have already been given directives to start its implementation. These priorities have boosted the morale of the administration and the officers involved. They will support the Government now for the speedy implementation of the action plan.

The positive attitude of the Government has sent a message that the Government means well and based on this impression, people look forward to good days ahead. Taking a cue from the mistakes made by UPA Government, Modi has directed his Ministers that they will not appoint any of their relatives as their personal staff in the Ministry and will not award any Government contracts to the relatives. He has also directed them to avoid wasteful expenditure on renovation and beautification of bungalows and offices. The issues raised by the State Governments must be given a priority and using Technology, peoples' complaints must be addressed on fast track.

Looking at the aggressive beginning made by Modi, the other members of the Ministry have also not spared any efforts to work hard. Everyone has started making ambitious plans for his department. With the promise of 'Good days', they have started the process of communication with the common masses in a speedy manner. Apart from asking for progress reports from various departments, Finance Minister Arun Jaitley has started serious discussions on Reforms in Taxation and strong and effective measures to contain inflation. Inflation and rising prices was a major issue in the elections which was raised by BJP with a lot of hue and cry. With this background, the Finance Minister will have to find out a robust solution. Minister of Foreign Affairs Sushma Swaraj seems to be very enthusiastic about her new portfolio,

It is commendable that Modi invited the heads of the neighboring countries and other heads of states for the swearing in ceremony and thus scored the first victory on the international diplomatic front. Sushma Swaraj said that the world can see India's strength now. We plan to improve our relationship with the neighbouring nations and strategic friends. This would a priority for the Government. After taking over the Health Ministry, Dr Harsh Vardhan immediately announced that Health Insurance coverage would be provided to everyone and people from all economic strata will be included in the National Health Insurance Scheme. The Urban Development Minister Venkaiah Naidu has promised homes for everyone by 2020 and to make home loans cheaper. Naidu is in favour of creating 100 smart cities. He wants to put an end to Jawaharlal Nehru Urban Renewal Mission and start a new programme. The Minister for Chemicals and Fertilizers Ananth Kumar has indicated to bring down the prices of essential medicines by 25 to 40 percent. Agriculture Minister Radha Mohan Singh talks of rural irrigation scheme for the entire country. Water Resources, River Development and Ganga Rejuvenation Minister Uma Bharati wants to lay special emphasis on cleansing of Ganga and she is preparing a plan for this.

All these plans pertaining to the progress of the nation are the gift of Modi's vision which the people of the nation are fervently praying for to succeed. Many people are also confused about the constitution of cabinet of Ministers. Analysts say that it is an outcome of his vision. A jumbo sized Ministerial cabinet cannot be a catalyst to progress. The size of the cabinet has been decided based on the concept of expediency.

Harishankar Vyas writes in Naya India that Modi's topmost priority is to achieve progress and development at a breakneck speed. He wants to make such fundamental differences in economic and administrative spheres which will make India a stiff competitor to other nations. It is for this reason he has given very important portfolios to the state Ministers with independent charge. The Responsibility of industrial development, infrastructure, mining, environment ministries is on the shoulder of young Ministers of State and an exercise to combine Transport and Shipping ministries has also been completed.

This structure means that the Prime Minister and his office will make things happen. The office of Prime Minister may undergo a sea change. Many do not know that the present form of the Prime Minister's office is far different than what it was during the time of Nehru and Shastri. During Nehru's time, there was Prime Minister's secretariat and not PMO office. There is a difference between PMO office and Prime Minister's secretariat. Today the PMO exists for administrative arrangements for PM, its stature and glitter. This has resulted in rendering the Cabinet Secretary and his office absolutely ineffective. Therefore, one of the ideas is to create a different structure of PM's secretariat along with PMO. It will keep an eye on Ministries, various happenings within the country and abroad, generate projects, monitor them and get results.

China and Japan operate in this manner. Therefore the plan to create a new structure for PM and his office is not an ordinary one. In this, the team formed in Delhi will work for PMO and the role of Modi's team in Gandhinagar will be decided as per the new plan of PM's secretariat. It would be interesting to see how Narendra Modi will effectively set up a structure manage his priorities with his active pre occupation of 18 to 20 hours in a day and how does he make use of Arun Shourie and his suggestions to prepare the blue print. The Chemistry between Arun Shourie and Modi will also decide if the Planning Commissions would continue or not. What further changes are required in the Ministry to make it more alert and which new innovative steps need to be taken to improve expediency?

The style of Modi's functioning certainly indicates that every day he will take some innovative decisions which would send a powerful and encouraging message to the masses, the slogan of 'Acche Din' is alive and being pursued seriously and Modi has not forgotten about it.

Modi's Cabinet of Ministers

Narendra Modi – **Prime Minister**

Other Ministries-Personnel, Public Grievances and Pensions, Department of Atomic Energy Department of Space, All important policy issues and all other portfolios not allocated to any Minister

Cabinet Ministers

1. Rajnath Singh –	Home Affairs
2. Sushma Swaraj –	External Affairs, Overseas Indian Affairs
3. Arun Jaitley –	Finance, Corporate Affairs, Defence
4. M Venkaiah Naidu –	Urban Development, Housing and Urban Poverty Alleviation, Parliamentary Affairs
5. Nitin Jayram Gadkari –	Road Transport and Highways, Shipping
6. D V Sadananda Gowda –	Railways
7. Uma Bharti –	Water Resources, River Development and Ganga Rejuvenation
8. Najma Heptullah –	Minority Affairs
9. Gopinath Munde –	Rural Development, Panchayati Raj, Drinking Water and Sanitation
10. Ramvilas Paswan –	Consumer Affairs, Food and Public Distribution
11. Kalraj Mishra –	Micro, Small and Medium Enterprises

12. Menaka Gandhi – Women and Child Development
13. Ananth Kumar – Chemicals and Fertilizers
14. Ravi Shankar Prasad – Communications and Information Technology, Law and Justice
15. Ashok Gajapathi Raju Pusapati – Civil Aviation
16. Anant Geete – Heavy Industries and Public Enterprises
17. Harsimrat Kaur Badal – Food Processing Industries
18. Narendra Singh Tomar – Mines, Steel, Labour and Employment
19. Jual Oram – Tribal Affairs
20. Radha Mohan Singh – Agriculture
21. Thaawar Chand Gehlot – Social Justice and Empowerment
22. Smriti Zubin Irani – Human Resource Development
23. Dr Harsh Vardhan – Health and Family Welfare

Ministers of State

1. General (Retd) V K Singh – Development of North Eastern Region (Independent Charge), External Affairs, Overseas Indian Affairs
2. Inderjit Singh Rao – Planning (Independent Charge), Statistics and Programme Implementation (Independent Charge), Defence
3. Santosh Kumar Gangwar – Textiles (Independent Charge), Parliamentary Affairs, Water Resources, River Development and Ganga Rejuvenation
4. Shripad Yesso Naik – Culture (Independent Charge), Tourism (Independent Charge)
5. Dharmendra Pradhan – Petroleum and Natural Gas (Independent Charge)
6. Sarbananda Sonowal – Skill Development, Entrepreneurship, Youth Affairs and Sports (Independent Charge)

7. Prakash Javadekar –	Information and Broadcasting (Independent Charge), Environment, Forest and Climate Change (Independent Charge), Parliamentary Affairs
8. Piyush Goyal –	Power (Independent Charge), Coal (Independent Charge), New and Renewable Energy (Independent Charge)
9. Jitendra Singh –	Science and Technology (Independent Charge), Earth Sciences (Independent Charge), Prime Minister Office, Personnel, Public Grievances & Pensions, Department of Atomic Energy, Department of Space
10. Nirmala Sitharaman –	Commerce and Industry (Independent Charge), Finance, Corporate Affairs
11. G M Siddeshwara –	Civil Aviation
12. Manoj Sinha –	Railways
13. Nihalchand –	Chemicals and Fertilizers
14. Upendra Kushwaha –	Rural Development, Panchayati Raj, Drinking Water and Sanitation
15. Radhakrishnan P –	Heavy Industries and Public Enterprises
16. Kiren Rijiju –	Home Affairs
17. Krishan Pal –	Road Transport and Highways, Shipping
18. Dr Sanjeev Kumar Balyan –	Agriculture, Food Processing Industries
19. Mansukhbhai Dhanjibhai Vasava –	Tribal Affairs
20. Raosaheb Dadarao Danve –	Consumer Affairs, Food and Public Distribution
21. Vishnu Deo Sai –	Mines, Steel, Labour and Employment
22. Sudarshan Bhagat –	Social Justice and Empowerment

Biography of Narendra Modi

1950 – 17th September Born at Vadnagar in Mehasana district

1962 – Worked in his father's tea stall at Vadnagar station. He served tea and offer hospitality to the soldiers passing through the station.

1965– He looked after the tea stall of his uncle at Ahmedabad ST bus stand. He came in contact with RSS workers there. Inspired by their patriotism, he decided to join RSS.

1968– Married Jashodaben. He left home on the first day after marriage after asking his wife to continue her studies.

1970– Kept wandering for two years. He went to Himalayas to meditate. Also went to Belur Math and lived there.

1975– He participated in the agitation during Emergency. He distributed the campaign literature and also helped the leaders who had participated in the agitation.

1987– He became the office bearer of All India Student Federation (Akhil Bharatiya Vidyarthi Parishad-ABVP). He became the General Secretary of BJP in Gujarat.

1990– He joined Advani in his Somnath chariot journey.

1995– He became the National Secretary of BJP and in-charge of 5 states.

1998– He became National General Secretary of BJP.

2001– He became the Chief Minister of Gujarat on 7th October.

2002– He faced all the allegations regarding the riots which broke out after the Godhra massacre. He contested the Legislative Assembly elections. He took over the administration of Gujarat as a Chief Minister for the second time.

2005– Denied visa to USA because of his alleged role in Gujarat riots.

2007– Modi becomes the Chief Minister for the third time.

2010– He gets a clean chit from the SIT constituted by Supreme Court.

2012– Hat-trick of win in Gujarat. Becomes the Chief Minister for the fourth time.

2013– On 13th September, BJP announces him as their candidate for the post of Prime Minister.

2014– Sworn in as the Prime Minister on 26th May.

References

We took help from many information media while writing this book. These include many newspapers, websites, TV channels and other resources. Major among these are:

Navbharat Times
Dainik Jagaran
Dainik Bhaskar
Rajasthan Patrika
Amar Ujala
Naya India
Navodaya Times
Rashtriya Sahara
Punjab Kesari
Zee News
ABP news
Aaj Tak
India Today
Outlook
Prabhat Khabar
BBC Hindi
Prabha sakshi
And many more